WORKING PAPERS NUMBER 5

ON THE OTHER: DIALOGUE AND/OR DIALECTICS

WORKING PAPERS NUMBER 5

Robert P. Scharlemann
Editor

ON THE OTHER: DIALOGUE AND/OR DIALECTICS

Mark Taylor's "Paralectics"

With Roy Wagner, Michael Brint, and Richard Rorty

UNIVERSITY
PRESS OF
AMERICA

Lanham • New York • London

COMMITTEE ON COMPARATIVE STUDY
OF INDIVIDUAL AND SOCIETY

Copyright © 1991 by
University Press of America®, Inc.
4720 Boston Way
Lanham, Maryland 20706

3 Henrietta Street
London WC2E 8LU England

Co-published by arrangement with the
Committee on the Comparative Study of the
Individual and Society of the Center for Advanced Studies
at the University of Virginia

Library of Congress Cataloging-in-Publication Data
On the Other : Dialogue and/or Dialectics :
Mark Taylor's Paralectics / with Roy Wagner, Michael Brint,
and Richard Rorty ; edited by Robert P. Scharlemann.
p.   cm. — (Working paper ; no. 5)
"Co-published by arrangement with the Center for
Advanced Studies"—T.p. verso.
Includes bibliographical references.
1. Literature—Philosophy.   2. Dialogue.   3. Religion
and postmodernism.   4. Dialectic.   I. Taylor, Mark
C., 1945-   II. Wagner, Roy.   III. Brint, Michael.
IV. Rorty, Richard.   V. Scharlemann, Robert P.
VI. Taylor, Mark. C., 1945- Paralectics.   1991.
VII. Series: Working papers (University of Virginia.
Committee on the Comparative Study of the
Individual and Society) ; no. 5.
PN49.O54   1991   110—dc20   91-31724 CIP

ISBN 1-8191-8382-2 (cloth : alk. paper)
ISBN 1-8191-8447-0 (paper : alk. paper)

 The paper used in this publication meets the minimum requirements of American National Standard for Information Sciences—Permanence of Paper for Printed Library Materials, ANSI Z39.48–1984.

CONTENTS

FOREWORD

R.S. KHARE

PROFESSOR OF ANTHROPOLOGY

UNIVERSITY OF VIRGINIA

The Committee on the Comparative Study of the Individual and Society occasionally publishes Working Papers on a theme or issue of sufficient interest to its members. Sometimes the Committee sponsored programs — occasional lectures, panel discussions, and colloquia — may also provide a basis for issuing a working paper. The purpose of these publications is to encourage wide ranging discussion of an issue within the University and outside. The readers of these papers are encouraged to share their ideas with authors and members of the Committee contributing to a particular working paper.

I
INTRODUCTION

ROBERT P. SCHARLEMANN
PROFESSOR OF RELIGIOUS STUDIES
UNIVERSITY OF VIRGINIA

A legend is told of two medieval monks who had agreed that the one of them who died first would send a message from the beyond. When, in the course of time, one of the monks died, the other monk directed a message to the deceased, asking whether the beyond was like the here. To his question came the reply "Nec taliter, nec aliter, sed totaliter aliter — neither the same, nor different, but totally different." This legend is not the direct source of the current discussion of otherness or alterity, nor even of Rudolf Otto's characterization of the numinous as "wholly other," but it indicates the nature of the problems involved in the discussion. The present volume of essays, which centers on Mark C. Taylor's "Paralectics," is occasioned by a question connected with the practice of conversation. In its most pointed form, it is the question of how (or whether) one can bring into a conversation someone whose being other seems to preclude that very possibility. Are there such other ones at all? Or are we entitled to assume that all human beings, and all things that in any way "speak," have enough in common to engage in a conversation about a theme? Taylor's essay raises the question in connection with Richard Rorty's philosophical hermeneutics. It asks whether Rorty's conception of dialogue is capable of taking adequate account of the other's being other. Rorty's own, spirited reply may be read either as an exhibition of the very problem Taylor's critique raises or as rejecting it. Whether it is to be read in the one way or the other is not for an editor's introduction to decide. But let us try to see the question at issue by beginning with the contrast between dialectic and dialogue that concerns Taylor.

The difference between dialogue and dialectic is the difference between Socrates and Hegel. In a dialogue, there is a certain openness and unpredictability of movement which seem to be precluded in a dialectic that moves from thesis to antithesis to resolution to further antithesis until every thinkable thesis has been brought into play. The goal of a final thesis may be unattainable, but the dialectical process is the same all through. A dialogue is much more disorderly. It involves surprises and turns that cannot be laid out in advance by a pattern, and partners in the dialogue do not purport to have in advance the criteria by which the matter under discussion is to be laid out or adjudicated. Indeed, a mark of genuine dialogue is that fact that the partners in it do in the course of the conversation come to see possibilities not anticipated. The zig-zag of such a dialogue is not the dialectic of thesis and antithesis. Now, Hegelian scholars may very well object that what we are speaking of as Hegelian dialectic here is as much a stereotype as it is a description of Hegel's own work. It might even be suggested that dialogue and dialectic are not possibilities so different as is indicated here. For Hegelian dialectic is not intended to describe the pattern of actual dialogue. It is meant to indicate, rather, the extreme points at which dialogue can take a turn. It is meant to say that, in any conversation, the basic (or extreme) turns are represented when the starting point is an unqualified assertion of a thesis and the next step an unqualified denial and the third step an absolute resolution. In actual conversation, such an assertion and its responses will actually encounter with many qualifications. But, if the conversation goes on long enough, one of its turns will be marked by the assertion of a direct antithesis of the thesis. ("Thesis" and "antithesis" are not distinctively Hegelian language, but they have become associated with him closely enough to be used especially of his form of dialectic.) *When* such an

2

antithetical assertion is made, the dialogue follows the pattern of a dialectic. Dialectic is, in other words, not intended to be an account of the way in which actual debate or conversation occurs but an account of the most basic turns that thought can take on a question. Dialectic need not be, indeed, should not be, closed in the sense of forcing all actual conversation into the pattern of affirmation, negation, and resolution (or limitation). It is rather the pattern which any actual conversation *can* follow when the most basic forms of its turns are exposed. Conversation does not require one of the interlocutors to assert a thesis for another interlocutor to contradict (as in a case argued in court or in formal debate); dialectical pattern means only that conversations, if carried on long enough, can move in such a way that the decisive turning points are related to each other like thesis and antithesis.

Nonetheless, even in this more open, or "softer," version of dialectic, there is the danger that attention is paid only to those moments in the conversation, or only to those participants in the conversation, at which the dialectical changes occur. Newspaper accounts of the public discourse are often of such a nature. They seek out the voices which represent the extreme opposite positions on a question and ignore the others. They do not trace the moments of an actual dialogue in the varieties and subtleties of many partners in a conversation but, instead, structure the conversation as though it were always a dialectic of Yes and No on a given question.

DIALECTIC RESOLUTION AND DIALOGICAL PAUSE

Taylor's question, however, is more subtle and precise than might be indicated by these general remarks on dialectic and dialogue. It has to do, first, with the nature of the transition from the one moment to the next in a conversation or dialectic. More specifically it has to do with the

3

movement beyond the conflict of contradictory opposites, the movement of resolution or of Hegelian *Aufhebung*. The key to the question is provided by Blanchot's observation, which Taylor notes, about the two kinds of pauses in a conversation. One pause is that of the change from one speaker to the next speaker. Unlike dialectical thought, which can be carried out by one person alone, a conversation depends upon two different persons. That difference is reflected in the dialogue by the pause, however slight, that accompanies the shift from one speaker to the other speaker. The second kind of pause is "the waiting that measures the distance between two interlocutors—no longer reducible distance, but the irreducible" (quoted by Taylor, p. 28). The first is the "pause that permits exchange" and the second is the "wait that measures infinite distance" (quoted by Taylor, p. 34). There could be no conversation, obviously, if the first interlocutor would never stop talking so as to allow the other interlocutor a chance to say something.

That stopping is the first kind of pause to which Blanchot refers. More significant for understanding Taylor's point is the second kind of pause. The "irreducible" or "infinite distance" between the two interlocutors refers to the way in which the one interlocutor can never say what the other says but can only listen to its being said by the other. The phenomenon to which Blanchot thus refers has everyday illustrations. We are all aware that certain ways of saying even familiar things may be perfectly acceptable grammatically and syntactically and yet they are locutions that we would never use ourselves — they are for others to use. We are also aware that our acquaintances have their ways of saying the familiar things and that it would surprise us if we heard them using other locutions. These common illustrations indicate the point that Blanchot is making, not only about the nature of conversations but also about the relation between discourse and its opposite. A radical pause is marked by "the refusal to discourse" that is "behind discourse" and the "refusal to

4

philosophize" that is "behind philosophy" (quoted by Taylor, p. 24), the *parole non parlante*. This is the aspect which, according to Taylor's critique, Rorty's hermeneutical philosophy does not include. Michael Brint, in his essay, questions whether this is an accurate reading of Rorty's hermeneutics, but he offers a criticism of that hermeneutics, under the title of American "romance," that may be another version of the same. The matter at issue is, in any case, the possibility of making listening to what the other has to say a part of the conversation. This not only includes listening to what initially sounds strange or wrong but becomes less strange when common ground is found; it also includes listening when we cannot appropriate what is being said because there is nothing common—listening to the one who, as it were, does nothing but interrupt the conversation. The core of Taylor's criticism of Rorty's conception of hermeneutics is that no such listening is possible if conversation is considered to be a way of self-edification; for then the other is reduced to an element in one's own becoming a self. This formulation of the criticism is not specifically discussed in the other essays, except for Rorty's brief dismissal of it; and this fact perhaps indicates that it needs some elaboration so that one can distinguish, for example, between using a conversation partner in order to upbuild one's own self, on the one hand, and, on the other hand, finding oneself changed as the result of listening to the other in a conversation. Then the question is whether Rorty's conception permits only the former.

For an answer to this question one would need to go beyond the contents of the present volume of essays. But Roy Wagner's essay, which treats of the difficulties encountered by anthropologists when they interpret the cultures they study, provides a concrete illustration of the importance of the question. As is clear from the essay, Wagner adopts into his "dif/ference" some of the same elements of Derridaian *différance* that Taylor has brought out in his essay, and, although he uses other imagery, his conception of the relation of dif/ference to the real differences among

5

cultures and to the differences among anthropologists' theories appears very much to be a concrete illustration of what Derrida and Taylor mean by the contrast between *différance* (and the Heideggerian *Unter-Schied* to which it is related), which is the deferring or setting apart that makes existing differences possible at all, and what is usually meant by difference.

It is not only anthropological researches into other cultures that are implicated in this question. Taylor's critique affects the matter of reading our own past as well. Is the attitude which Rorty describes as one that is "interested not so much in what is out there in the world, or what happened in history, as in what we can get out of nature and history for our own uses" (quoted by Taylor, p. 16) an attitude of not listening to the other? Do history and nature present us with materials that can, as it were, disrupt our uses of nature and history in the way that an interrupting voice can disrupt the course of a dialogue? These questions received less attention that they might have in the several essays.

DIALECTIC AND SUBORDINATION

As both Brint and Wagner bring out, there is a political aspect to the whole matter too. Taylor's question thus has to do, in the second place, with the way in which dialectic is joined with the themes of hierarchy and subordination. The connection is made more by allusion and mention than by explanation in Taylor's essay. But it is not difficult to see how dialectic and political subordination can be akin to each other. If the dialectical movement, unlike an open conversation, does not involve listening to what is inappropriate and unappropriable, then everything must be given its proper place in the scheme of things by the dialectical pattern itself. More than that, the implication of dialectical resolution is that the third element in the dialectic includes the preceding elements in itself. The resolution is

6

always a more advanced stage than the opposites in their opposition to each other. In his philosophy of history, Hegel can thus trace the advance of freedom from societies in which only one person is free to those in which all are free and from those in which the freedom of all is an abstract liberty of individuals to those in which it is concrete, i.e., in harmony with the social whole. The synthesis always includes the thesis and the antithesis while eliminating, as Hegel put it, the form of opposition between them. If this is so, then those who live in a society in which all are free, especially those who are the theorists of such a society, have something to tell to other societies, in which only one or some are free, but do not have much to learn from them. If other societies are those which have not yet advanced to the stage of development of free society, the notion that free societies should listen and learn from those other societies becomes at best problematic.

Whether Rorty's notion of the open-ended conversation is subject to this criticism is judged differently by the essayists here. Rorty replies to the criticism in his own way, suggesting—if one may put it in general terms —that there are indeed certain advances which, despite what we might say to the contrary, we take unquestionably as advances (p. 74). Brint seems less certain of the case. Although he thinks Taylor's is partly a misreading of Rorty's position, he reaches a similar result from a different direction when he suggests that Rorty has ironically offered "yet another romantic presentation of good texts over bad texts" (p. 66).

EDITORIAL PRIVILEGE

It is not usually the role of an editor to intervene in the discussion of the essays being published. Since the present editor, however, thinks he knows something about Tillich's theology, he finds it irresistible to make a correction of Rorty's account of Tillich in a point on which Tillich is

7

frequently misrepresented. Tillich did not "brush aside Heidegger's identification of philosophical research with atheism" (p. 72). Along with Rudolf Bultmann, though before he had ever read or probably heard of Heidegger, Tillich had taken the position that it is not philosophy's task or nature to have anything to say for or against God; in that sense philosophical research is and ought to be atheist. Tillich did distinguish between "autonomous" and "theonomous" philosophies, but the distinction between the two did not have to do with whether they were theistic or atheistic nor did it imply that philosophical or scientific research could or should be anything but unconcerned about theism and atheism. Heidegger's philosophy was, in Tillich's judgment, "theonomous" (and not only "autonomous") but it was not theistic.

The direction in which the influences flowed at Marburg in the 1920s may be hard to pin down exactly, so that it may be difficult to tell how much Heidegger got from Bultmann (the best known of the early Heideggerian theologians) or other Marburg theologians and how much they got from Heidegger. In some matters the direction seems clear—it is hard, for example, to imagine that Heidegger's account of the contemporary state of theology given in *Being and Time* §3 was not the result of what he had learned from the Marburg theologians. In other matters the direction of influence may not be so clear. Were Bultmann and Heidegger about the same time making a theme of the atheism of modern science because the one had got the idea from the other? In Tillich's case, it is clear that Tillich was talking about "being" (never capitalized in Tillich's English) before he had read Heidegger; and even in the later *Systematic Theology*, which correlates "the question of being" with "the symbol of God," the correlative terms *God* and *being* can never be conflated. There is, indeed, a traceable change in Tillich's understanding of "being" and a change that is clearly due to his becoming acquainted with Heidegger's concept of being.[1] There, as elsewhere, it is plain that

8

whatever might otherwise be said of him, Tillich did not "relabel" as God what Heidegger called "being." Even at the risk of editorial impropriety (or, let us say, through an editorial interruption), this is a correction worth making since Tillich is so often misrepresented in the literature.

But enough of editorial interruptions. The reader is to be invited to read the essays themselves.

NOTES

1. The tracing can be done by reference to *The System of the Sciences According to Objects and Methods* (1923), where it is clear that Tillich uses "ontology" in a sense quite different from Heidegger's, and to *Die Gestalt der Religiösen Erkenntnis* (unpublished, but not earlier than 1926), in which the prologue clearly reflects a debate with Heidegger's sense of ontology and being. In this latter case, God is not equated with being but with "the beyond of being."

II
PARALECTICS[1]

MARK C. TAYLOR

WILLIAMS COLLEGE

The city rat invites the country rat onto the Persian rug. They gnaw and chew leftover bits of ortolan. Scraps, bits and pieces, leftovers: their royal feast is only a meal after a meal among the dirty dishes of a table that had not been cleared. ... It's nighttime, black. What happens would be the obscure converse of clear and conscious organization, happening behind everyone's back, the dark side of the system. But what do we call these nocturnal processes? Are they destructive or constructive? Are they the exception or the genesis? What happens at night on the rug covered with crumbs? Is it a still active trace of (an) origin? Or is it only a remaining margin [*marge restant*] of missing suppressions? We can, undoubtedly, decide the matter: the battle [*la battaille*] against rats is already lost; there is no house, ship, or place that does not have its share. There is no system without parasites.

(Michael Serres)

The questions with which I would like to linger are posed by the discourse of the other. Does the other speak? Can I (the "I") hear/understand (*entends*) the other? Who or what is the other ... the other that approaches (without arriving) as the not-same? Is the other who is my counterpart actually other or is s/he really identical in her/his difference? "Is" there an other other that allows others to be other and differences to be different? How might such an other be (almost) thought? Does the other other make any difference ... or every difference?

To linger with questions posed by the discourse of the other is to wrestle with the problem of translation. Can the other speak *my* language? Can I *make* the other speak *my* language? Can I speak an other or the other's language? Does translation allow the other to speak or does it silence the discourse of the other? Without translation, there is no conversation—no shared communication. And yet, can either *entretien* or *partager* be translated with certainty?

Entretien: conversation, talk, interview.

Entretenir: to hold together, keep in good order; to maintain, support, feed; to converse or talk with, to entertain.

Entre, between + *tenir*, to hold.

Entretien: a holding-between.

Partage: sharing, distribution, division; share, lot, portion, apportionment.

Partager: *diviser*; *démember, morceler*; *couper, fractionner, fragmenter*; *solidariser*; *participer*. To divide, share out; to share, participate in.

11

Share: the iron blade in a plough that cuts the ground at the bottom of the furrow. From *(s)ker*, scratch, cut, pluck, gather, dig, separate, sift; and *sek*, divide, cut, scrape.

Share: a part or portion belonging to, distributed to, contributed by, or owned by a person or group; to divide, parcel out in shares; to apportion, participate in use, or experience in common.

Partage parts and divides by be(com)ing the converse of itself. Forever suspended *entre-deux, le partage des voix* marks the re-turn of *l' entretien infini*.

ART OF CONVERSATION

... granted that Derrida is the latest and largest flower on the dialectical kudzu vine of which the *Phenomenology of Spirit* was the first tendril, does that not merely show the need to uproot this creeping menace? Can we not now see all the better the need to strip the suckers of this parasitic climber from the still unfinished walls and roofs of the great Kantian edifice which it covers and conceals?[2]

(Richard Rorty, "Philosophy as a Kind of Writing")

In a series of articles and books written over the past decade Richard Rorty has been developing an interpretation of conversation—or more precisely an interpretation of interpretation in terms of conversation—that has become extremely influential. The impact of Rorty's work has been both widespread and significant. For many, the recent turn in Rorty's

12

thinking signals a renewed openness of philosophy to broader issues that are being discussed in other fields of inquiry. To others, Rorty seems to have fallen prey to the temptations of decadent postmodernism. For many of Rorty's erstwhile philosophical colleagues, the scandal seems to be that one of the most respected members of their congregation has committed heresy by falling under the spell of illusions from which true believers have long been free. When one recalls that contemporary Anglo-American linguistic philosophy began as reaction to the revival of Hegelianism in England during the early decades of this century, the impact of Rorty's "fall" becomes more understandable. In shedding his analytical skin, Rorty has had the audacity to argue that Hegel, if read in a certain way, was right. To make matters worse, Rorty (mistakenly, in my judgment) maintains that the return to Hegel via Gadamer makes it possible to appropriate important insights from contemporary philosophers who have to be anathematized by the high priests of the philosophical ecclesia. Rorty's errancy, however, is neither as extreme as his detractors insist nor as radical as his supporters believe.

Acknowledging that he stands in the tradition of the *Phenomenology of Spirit*, Rorty suggests, albeit inadvertently, the way in which his philosophy extends the Western struggle to master difference. Instead of patiently listening to a discourse not his own, Rorty's "dialogue" actually ends in a monologue spoken/written to colonize the other. In the aftermath of this conversation, a persistent question remains: Is it ever possible to break the circle of domination by overcoming the domination of the (hermeneutical) circle?

As one skilled in the art of conversation, Rorty likes to tell stories. His reading of the story of modern philosophy has only two chapters, which are variously described as epistemology and hermeneutics or commensuration and conversation. As his use of the image of the parasitic kudzu vine suggests, Rorty traces these two types of philosophy back to

Kant and Hegel respectively. Though epistemology and hermeneutics differ significantly in assumptions and conclusions, the most important differences distinguishing them can best be seen in their alternative accounts of representation. "The [Kantian] tradition thinks of truth as a vertical relationship between representation and what is represented. The [Hegelian] tradition thinks of truth horizontally—as the culminating reinterpretation of our predecessors' reinterpretation of their predecessor' reinterpretation.... This tradition does not ask how representations are related to nonrepresentations, but how representations can be seen as hanging together. The difference is not one between "correspondence" and "coherence" theories of truth.... Rather, it is the difference between regarding truth, goodness, and beauty as eternal objects which we try to locate and reveal, and regarding them as artifacts whose fundamental design we often have to alter."[3]   While "Kantianism" struggles to re-present primal presentations, "Hegelianism" acknowledges the inaccessibility of every thing-in-itself and admits that representations always refigure representations. In the absence of primal presentation, signs are signs of signs.

As I have noted, this (all too) neat-and-tidy philosophical tale makes sense *only* if Hegel is read in a certain way. It is significant that Rorty's genealogy goes back to the *Phenomenology of Spirit* rather than the System. For Rorty, there is a significant difference between the implications of the phenomenological and the systematic Hegel. In the *Encyclopedia of the Philosophical Sciences*, Hegel claims to have reached absolute knowledge by accurately representing the truth that had been gradually unfolding in nature and history from the beginning of time. The *Phenomenology*, by contrast, examines the experience of consciousness as it moves from subjective self-certainty to the truth that is purportedly (re)present(ed) in the System as a whole. Repeating insights advanced by earlier commentators, Rorty describes the *Phenomenology* as a

Bildungsroman in which each chapter is, in effect, a rewriting of earlier chapters in the genesis of self-consciousness.[4] Over against Hegel, Rorty insists that the final chapter of the story cannot be written and thus a conclusive end is forever delayed. The deferral of absolute knowledge creates the possibility of an unending conversation that is essentially hermeneutical. From this point of view, hermeneutics can be understood as something like Hegelianism without absolute knowledge. "Hermeneutics," Rorty explains, "sees the relations between various discourses as those of strands in a possible conversation, a conversation which presupposes no disciplinary matrix which unites the speakers, but where the hope of agreement is never lost so long as the conversation lasts. This hope is not a hope for the discovery of antecedently existing common ground, but *simply* hope for agreement, or, at least, exciting and fruitful disagreement."[5] While epistemology is an archeological search for secure foundations, hermeneutics is a teleological quest for a certainty that never arrives. Rorty is persuaded that only when conversation gives up the dream of commensuration can it become edifying.

Though Hegel repeatedly asserts that philosophy can never edify, Rorty insists on "translating" Hegelian *Bildung* into hermeneutical *edification.*[6] Edification involves the process of building up oneself in and through the expansion of consciousness and self-consciousness brought about by "acculturation."[7] In Rorty's philosophical story, Gadamer emerges as a pivotal character. By successfully extricating the notion of *Bildung* from the most problematic metaphysical presuppositions of nineteenth-century idealism, Gadamer prepares the way for the recognition of the thoroughgoing historicity of human consciousness. Commenting on *Truth and Method*, Rorty writes:

... the importance of Gadamer's book is that he manages to separate off one of the three strands—the romantic notion of

15

man as self-creative—in the philosophical notion of "spirit" from the other two strands with which it became entangled. Gadamer... makes no concessions either to Cartesian dualism or to the notion of "transcendental constitution." He thus helps to reconcile the "naturalistic" point... that the "irreducibility of the *Geisteswissenschaften*" is not a matter of metaphysical dualism... with our "existentialist" intuition that redescribing ourselves is the most important thing we can do. He does this by substituting the notion of *Bildung* (education, self-formation) for that of "knowledge" as the goal of thinking. To say that we become different people, that we "remake" ourselves as we read more, talk more, and write more, is simply a dramatic way of saying that the sentences which become true of us by virtue of such activities are often more important to us than sentences which become true of us when we drink more, eat more, and so on.[8]

In Hegel's metanarrative, history is the process in which the absolute subject (*Geist*) becomes self-conscious through the emergence of total self-consciousness in individual subjects. With the disappearance of the absolute subject, history becomes anthropocentric. "Gadamer," Rorty argues, "develops his notion of *wirkungsgeschichtliches Bewusstein* (the sort of consciousness of the past which changes us) to characterize an attitude interested not so much in what is out there in the world, or in what happened in history, as in what we can get out of nature and history for our own uses."[9]

When attempting to assess the implications of Rorty's account of *Bildung*, it is important not to overlook his use of phrases like: "self-formation", "man as self-creative", "we "remake" ourselves as we read more, talk more, and write more", and, most surprisingly, "an attitude

16

interested not so much in what is out there in the world, or in what happened in history, as in what we can get out of nature and history for our own uses." Firmly rooted in the Western humanist tradition, Gadamer declares that "like nature, *Bildung* has no goals outside itself."[10] So understood, *Bildung* is the auto-telic process in which subjects perpetually remake themselves through ongoing interrelationships. Since "the point of edifying philosophy is to keep the conversation going rather than to find objective truth," hermeneutics is "the infinite *striving for* truth over "all of Truth.""[11] The striving subject enters into conversation in order to build *itself* up through the search for truth. Thus the person who converses relates to *herself/himself* even when s/he seems to be relating to others. In one of his most revealing remarks about edification, Rorty explains: "for edifying discourse is *supposed* to be abnormal, to take us out of our old selves by the power of strangeness, to aid us in becoming new beings."[12] From this hermeneutical point of view, we enter relationship with the "others" in order to become "new beings." The relation to the "other" is, therefore, a self-relation that is self-transforming. The "other" is not really other but is actually a *moment* in *my* own self-becoming. The trick of conversation is to turn around (i.e., con-verse) in such a way that one rediscovers *self* in other.

Rorty is led to this understanding of hermeneutics by his acceptance of Gadamer's claim that *play* provides the proper model for interpreting interpretation. The Gadamerian notion of play that Rorty appropriates exposes the idealistic assumptions and conclusions that plague hermeneutics. In the Preface to the *Phenomenology*, Hegel describes the life of the divine, which, it is important to remember, is concretely incarnate in the life of each individual subject, in terms of play.

The life of God and divine cognition may well be spoken of as a play of love with itself; but this idea sinks into edification, even insipidity, if it lacks the seriousness, the suffering, the patience, and the labor of the negative.[13]

Hegel's account of play extends the analysis advanced by Schiller in *On the Education of Man* and elaborated by Kant in the interpretation of the work of art presented in the *Critique of Judgment*.[14] The essential feature of play for Hegel is its self-reflexivity. Inasmuch as play is always self-contained, players actually never relate to anything or anyone other than themselves.

As Hegel emphasizes, it is a mistake to view play as simply light-hearted or frivolous activity. Genuine play is impossible apart form what Hegel describes as "the labor of the negative." Dialectical negativity is not merely negative but is also positive. The negative becomes positive when it is doubled. The structure of the Hegelian dialectic is double negation in which negation first emerges and then is negated. Double negation reconciles what appears to be merely negative (e.g., difference or otherness) by incorporating it within a comprehensive totality that is essentially positive. In terms of the development of self-consciousness, Hegel maintains that to become itself, the subject must enter into relation with others in such a way that their differences become constitutive of the subject's own being. Since relation to other is requisite for self-identity, the other is not simply other but is at the same time also one's own self. Self-consciousness presupposes the re-cognition of self in other. The relation to the other is, therefore, a necessary moment in the building up of the subject's own identity. Though Hegel rejects the term "edification," his *Bildungsroman* anticipates Rorty's contention that we enter into conversation with others "to aid us in becoming new beings."

The link joining Hegel's *Bildung* and Rorty's edification is Gadamer's aesthetics of play. In *Truth and Method*, Gadamer argues that "the concept of play" is "the clue to the ontological explanation of the work of art and its hermeneutical significance." Indirectly recalling Kant's description of the work of art in terms of inner teleology, Gadamer approaches the aesthetic object through the notion of *representation* implied in play. "Play," he argues, "is really limited to representing *itself*. Thus its mode of being is *self-representation*."[15] To say that play "is self-representation," is to say that play *must* be purposeless or, more precisely, must have no purpose outside of itself. As soon as we play for a reason we are not playing but working. Since play never points beyond itself it represents nothing other than itself. For Gadamer, as for his precursors, play is essentially self-referential or self-reflexive.

Play, of course, becomes actual only through the activity of individual players. As Gadamer points out, "the self-representation of the game involves the player's achieving, as it were, his own self-representation by playing, i.e., representing something. Only because play is always representation is human play able to find the task of the game in representation itself."[16] Inasmuch as play is *self*-re-present-ation, its privileged time is the *present*, or, in Gadamer's terms, "a present time sui generis." Play re-presents itself in representative players. When play is satisfying, players become present to themselves in the act of re-presenting play itself. In this way, the self-representation of play creates the possibility of the self-presentation of players.

The self-presence of the player is not simple but is unavoidably complex. Having been taken up into the self-representation of play, the player can become present to herself/himself only in and through another player. For this reason, Gadamer insists that "to be present is to share."[17] When sharing, one no longer seems bound up within oneself but appears to be integrally related to another person. If, as Gadamer avers, to be

19

present is to share, then, "to be present, as a subjective act of a human attitude, has the character of being outside of oneself."[18] Presence, in other words, is ecstasy (*ek-stasis*). The exteriority with which the subject that is "outside" of itself is involved is not, however, radical but is a covert interiority waiting to be discovered. In Hegelian terms, true self-representation presupposes the negation of negation through which the universal realizes itself in the particular and the particular realizes itself in the universal. In theological terms, the self must lose itself to gain *itself*. Summarizing his analysis of play as the model for the hermeneutical significance of the ontology of the work of art, Gadamer explicitly invokes the theological language implicit in his entire argument.

Thus to the ecstatic self-forgetfulness of the spectator there corresponds his continuity with himself. Precisely that in which he loses himself as a spectator requires his own continuity. It is the truth of his own world, the religious and moral world in which he lives, which presents itself to him and in which he recognizes himself. Just as the parousia, absolute presence, describes the ontological mode of aesthetic being, and a work of art is the same whenever it becomes such a presence, so the absolute moment in which a spectator stands is at once self-forgetfulness and reconciliation with self. That which detaches him from everything also gives him back the whole of his being.[19]

Sharing is the redemptive *telos* of the hermeneutical enterprise. One enters into conversation or dialogue with an other—be that other historical, i.e., a subject that was present in the past, or a contemporary—in order to establish a self-realizing communion/communication. The parousia arrives (albeit momentarily) when horizons *fuse* to create (holy) communion.

To reach an understanding with one's partner in a dialogue is not merely a matter of total self-expression and the successful assertion of one's own point of view, but a transformation into a communion, in which we do not remain what we were.[20]

When dialogue becomes "a communion, in which we do not remain what we were," conversation is truly edifying. Edifying discourse involves a sharing that unites rather than divides, joins rather than separates.

While acknowledging that conversation is *l'entretien infini*, hermeneutical interpretations of dialogue, like those developed by Gadamer and Rorty, entail a one-sided reading of *le Partage des Voix*.[21] As I have stressed, "to share" means not only to participate in use, or experience in common, but also to divide and distribute. By reading *part* in *partage*, it becomes possible to hear the converse of hermeneutical conversation. Rorty (like Hegel and Gadamer before him) remains deaf to this alternative discourse. This deafness is not accidental but is "the blind spot," which, paradoxically, allows the hermeneutical philosopher to see. Why does the hermeneut who is preoccupied with hearing and seeing nonetheless remain deaf and blind? Why can s/he neither see nor hear the other as other? Why does hermeneutical dialogue tend to turn into a complex monologue? The answer to these and related questions might be found in a different interpretation of play. Suppose play does not issue in presence or re-presentation but stages their impossibility.

In an extremely influential essay entitled "Structure, Sign, and Play," Derrida claims: "Play is the disruption of presence."[22] Rorty does not seem to hear the point Derrida is making. The reason for this failure lies in Rorty's insistence that "to understand Derrida, one must see his work as the latest development of this non-Kantian [i.e., Hegelian] tradition—the latest attempt of the dialecticians to shatter the Kantians' ingenuous image

21

of themselves as accurately representing how things really are."[23] While Hegel exposes the Kantian thing-in-itself as a covert concept, Derrida demonstrates that what seems to be outside any text is inescapably bound up in textual play. Derridean textualism is, according to Rorty, "the contemporary counterpart of idealism."[24] This is not to imply that Rorty believes that Derrida simply repeats Hegel. To the contrary, he realizes that "for Derrida, writing always leads to more writing, and more, and still more—just as history does not lead to Absolute Knowledge or to the Final Struggle, but to more history, and more, and still more. The *Phenomenology's* vision of truth as what you get by reinterpreting all the previous reinterpretations of reinterpretations still embodies the Platonic ideal of the Last Reinterpretation, the *right* interpretation at last. Derrida wants to keep the horizontal character of Hegel's notion of philosophy without its teleology, its sense of direction, its seriousness."[25]

Rorty claims that this "deconstructed" Hegel without teleology is virtually indistinguishable from the hermeneutical Hegel whose infinite striving never reaches the end. It is, of course, true that Derrida frequently asserts that absolute knowledge is forever delayed or deferred. Derridean deferral, however, differs significantly from hermeneutical postponement. Derrida's textualism entails a more radical critique of representation than either Gadamer's or Rorty's hermeneutics. Since he misreads Derrida as a dialectical thinker who, in spite of important differences, remains in the Hegelian tradition, Rorty fails to grasp the differences between the hermeneutical and the deconstructive critiques of representation. In both hermeneutics and deconstruction, reality as such or things-in-themselves can never be represented. From a deconstructive point of view, however, hermeneutics remains committed to a philosophy of presence that is repressive of difference and otherness. In self-referential dialogue and auto-telic conversation, the *structure* of representation persists as the self-reflexive process in which subjects become present to themselves in each

22

other and remain identical with themselves in every difference. All dialogue/conversation is dialectical insofar as difference is negated and otherness sublated. The speaking subject, it seems, always *dictates*.

Hermeneutics, in other words, remains caught up in the circle of presence and plenitude. Though the *total* presence of the plenitude of meaning might forever be deferred, dialectical conversation always transpires within the horizon of presence and re-presentation. The absence of "the transcendental signified" is the condition of the *possibility* of hope in eschatological self-presence. By contrast, the "play" in "Structure, Sign and Play" announces a "*rupture*" with the entire economy of presence and representation. For Derrida, the "absence" (but this is a curious absence) of the transcendental signified is the condition of the *impossibility* of plenary self-presence in any temporal modality—i.e., past, present, or future. As the disruption of presence, "play is always play of absence and presence, but if it is to be thought radically, play must be conceived of before the alternative of presence and absence."[26] That which "is" *before* the alternative of presence and absence, and thus is properly neither present nor absent, opens the uncanny time-space for an other discourse, that might be the dis-course of the other. Derrida observes:

> Here there is a kind of question, let us still call it historical, whose *conception, formation, gestation,* and *labor* we are only catching a glimpse of today. I employ these words, I admit, with a glance toward the operations of childbearing—but also with a glance toward those who, in a society from which I do not exclude myself, turn their eyes away when faced by this as yet unnameable which is proclaiming itself and which can still do so, as is necessary whenever a birth is in the offing, only under the species of

nonspecies, in the formless, mute infant, and terrifying form of monstrosity.[27]

The (always) as yet unnameable can be spoken/written, if at all, only "in"

OUTLINES

Must we always talk in circles... circles that tend to be hermeneutical? Are outlines impossible? Or do outlines sketch the impossibility inscribed by the *Riss* of *Umriss*? Might the *Riss* rending *Umriss* imply, in Maurice Blanchot's words, "something that will not find itself in any text, the outside of the text [*hors texte*], the superfluous word, word too much [*le mot de trop*], in order that it not be wanting with respect to the completeness of complete Works, or to the contrary that it should always want"?[28] The *hors-texte... mot de trop* breaks the hermeneutical circle by interrupting every conversation.

Behind discourse speaks the refusal to discourse, as behind philosophy would speak the refusal to philosophize: non-speaking speech [*la parole nonparlante*], violent, concealing, saying nothing and suddenly crying.[29]

La parole non parlante is a word that divides as much as it unites, separates as well as joins. Neither simply binding nor unbinding, *le mot de trop* is always *entre-deux*—suspended (in the) between. Forever falling between the lines, *la parole non parlante* echoes in (empty) space or nonspace that cannot be represented but can, at best, be outlined. The dis-course of this strange word, which both haunts and eludes hermeneutical conversation, repeatedly returns to fragment Blanchot's extraordinary *L'Entretien Infini*

24

and to disrupt Jean-Luc Nancy's provocative *Le Partage des Voix*. What Gadamer and Rorty struggle to repress, Blanchot and Nancy attempt to solicit.

Near the end of *Le Partage des Voix*, Nancy notes that somewhere Heidegger asks: "Is dialogue necessarily a dialectic and when?"[30] The task Nancy sets for himself is to reread Heidegger's interpretation of language and the hermeneutical circle through Blanchot's analysis of *l'entretien* so as to establish the possibility of nondialectical dialogue. Though Nancy never puts it in these terms, to entertain a nondialectical notion of dialogue, it is necessary to develop a nonlogocentric reading of language. While Heidegger remains caught in the logocentrism of the ontotheological tradition whose end he nonetheless tolls, some of his most interesting writings outline an account of language that points toward (but does not represent) that which escapes the hermeneutical circle. Heidegger develops an alternative account of language by rethinking language in terms of *Unterschied*—difference or distinction. In a text entitled *Unterwegs zur Sprache*, he writes:

Language speaks. It speaks by bidding the bidden, thing-world and world-thing, to come to the between of difference. What is so bidden is commanded to arrive from out of the difference into the dif-ference.... The dif-ference gathers the two out of itself as it calls them into the rift that is the dif-ference.[31]

From Heidegger's point of view, semantics and syntax, which usually are taken to be the essence of language, are secondary to a more originary play of differences that forever escapes nomination. In this context, language is not a means of communication by which decipherable messages are sent and received. Rather, language articulates the opening—the between—that

25

makes possible all "comm-*uni*-cation" (*communicare*, to make common). As such, language is antecedent to and escapes from the communicative acts it enables to transpire. Since it entails a double rhythm, language is irreducibly duplicitous. While language holds together contraries usually set apart, it also holds apart the opposites it brings together. The mean that both joins and separates is dif-ference. It is important not to confuse *Unter-Schied* with any particular difference. Heidegger's dif-ference articulates the differences that constitute language in the ordinary sense of the term. This marginal dif-ference is the tear that both enables and interrupts all discourse. Though the *Riss* of *Unter-Schied* creates the clearing in which the hermeneutical circle can be drawn, no circle can contain this *hors texte.*[32]

    Nancy and Blanchot are obsessed with the tear of dif-ference. Heideggerian dif-ference, Nancy argues, forever eludes the (dialectical and binary) opposites it articulates. The *Riss* of *Unter-Schied* is a radical difference that can never be reduced to identity and a wholly other that cannot be returned to the same. While dialectical (i.e., hermeneutical) dialogue is either deaf to, or tries to silence every such difference, nondialectical dialogue solicits an other it can neither contain nor express. In a footnote devoted to Heidegger's use of *Gespräche* (conversation, discourse, dialogue), Nancy underscores the inescapable duplicity of *partage.*

    Le *Gespräche* implies a *Ge-flecht* (netting, lattice texture; *Flechte*, plait tress; twist, braid; *flechten*, twist, interweave, intertwine) or is grasped in *Ge-flecht.* Perhaps it would be necessary to say that *Geflecht* is that which is given the regime or nature of the *Ge* of *Gespräch*: that is to say, a "collective" (this is the ordinary nature of the *Ge-*), but with the function of a *between* [*entretien*]), and finally of a *dia-* that does not dialectise but that shares [*partage*]. That which interweaves us divides us, that which divides us interweaves us.[33]

Since conversation not only joins but also separates, *le partage des voix* "indicates the finitude of dialogue, that is to say, again, not the limited status of all actual dialogues, based on an infinite dialogue, but this—that the essence of dia-logue is in the infinite alteration of the other [*l'altération infinie de l'autre*]."[34] Paradoxically, dialogue is infinite precisely because it is finite.

The *infini* of *l'entretien infini* cannot be represented but can only be stages or performed *indirectly*—as if "in" outline(s). Language is never only itself but is always at the same time the discourse of the other, which, as *le mot de trop*, remains in a certain sense unspeakable. The converse of dialectical/hermeneutical conversation repeatedly returns to interrupt the communication whose space it nonetheless clears.[35] Since the eternal return of the discourse of the other is inevitably differential, *la parole* is *la parole plurielle*.[36] In an important section of *L'Entretien Infini* entitled *L'interruption*, Blanchot describes alternative approaches to (or of) interruption.

Interruption is necessary to every sequence of words. Intermittence renders becoming possible; discontinuity assures continuity of understanding, from which there certainly would be much to infer. But for the moment I would like to show that this intermittence by which discourse becomes dialogue, that is to say dis-course, presents itself in two very different ways.

27

In the first case, the arrest-interval [*l'arrêt-intervalle*] is comparable to the ordinary pause that permits the "taking turns" of a conversation [*entretien*]. Discontinuity, then, is essential, since it promises exchange; essential but relative: what it alludes to is, had it been late or never, and at the same time as early as today, the affirmation of unitary truth, where coherent discourse will no longer cease, and no longer ceasing, will confound itself with its silent inverse. From this perspective, rupture, even if it fragments, opposes, or disturbs common speech, still serves its interest. Not only does it confer meaning, but it disengages common meaning as horizon. It is the respiration of discourse. All forms that depend on dialectical experience of existence and history—from quotidian babble to the highest moments of reason, struggle, and practice—would fall in this category. To interrupt oneself in order to understand oneself/one another [*s'interrompre pour s'entendre*].

But there is another kind of interruption, more enigmatic and more critical [*grave*]. It introduces the waiting that measures the distance between two interlocutors—no longer reducible distance, but the irreducible.[37]

The play of this *other* interruption—*l'éntrangeté... l'autre... infiniment séparé... fissure... intervalle... endehors de moi... altérité... l'inconnu dans son infinie distance*—is the play of altarity. In the strangeness of this interval, fissure, tear, *Riss*, Blanchot thinks play radically—"before the alternative of presence and absence."[38] This *Jeu* is an other play... a play that is the "monstrous" play of the other.

28

In the play of Blanchot's *entretien*, speech, the word says: "infinite distance and difference, distance that is attested in *la parole* itself and that holds it outside of all contestation, all parity and all commerce."[39] *L'entretien* maintains (*tient*) the between (*entre*) without which there can be no conversation and with which there can be neither unification nor communication.

> When I appeal to the Other, I respond to that which speaks to me from no place and am separated from it by a caesura such that the Other forms with me neither a duality nor a unity. It is this fissure—this relation with the other—which we have dared to characterize as an interruption of being, now adding: between man and man there is an interval that would be neither of being nor of non-being, carried by the Difference of speech, a difference that precedes everything different and everything unique.[40]

The "between" (*l'entre-deux*), which is neither positive nor negative, neither is nor is not, is a difference or an other that cannot be dialectically sublated through the duplicitous positivity of double negation. Repeatedly slipping away from the dialectical logic of both/and, as well as the anti-dialectical logic of either/or, the timely interval of *l'intretien* implies the paralogic of the neither/nor.

> *between: between/ne(u)ter.* Play, play without the happiness of playing, with this residue of a letter that would appeal to the night with the lure of a negative presence. The night radiates the night as far as the neuter, where the night extinguishes itself.[41]

29

The paralogic of the neuter can be figured, if at all, only in paralectics. A paralectic parodies a dialectic by miming the communication of that which is incommunicable. As such, every paralectic is parasitic upon a dialectic. Conversely, each dialectic is parasitic upon a paralectic to which it must remain deaf if messages are to be sent and received. *Neither* both/and *nor* either/or, the paralogic of paralectics figures a neuter that simultaneously creates the space for dialogue and neutralizes the transparency of the signs exchanged.

Something is at work on the part of the neuter, which is in the same instant the work of idleness [*désoeuvrement*]. There is an effect of the neuter, or a neuter effect—called the passivity of the neuter—which is not the effect *of* the neuter, not being the effect of a Neuter supposedly at work as cause or thing. There would not be therefore a labor of the neuter, as one says: labor of the negative. The Neuter, paradoxical name: it hardly speaks, mute word, simple, yet always veiling itself, always displacing itself outside of its meaning, operating invisibly on itself and not ceasing to uncoil itself, in the immobility of its position which repudiates depth. It neutralizes, neutralizes (itself), and thereby evokes (does nothing but evoke), the movement of *Aufhebung*; but if it suspends and retains, it retains only the movement of suspension, that is to say, the distance that it suscitates by the fact that, in occupying the terrain, it makes the distance disappear. The Neuter designates, then, the difference in indifference, the opacity in transparency, the negative scansion of the other which can only reproduce itself by the conjured—omitted—attraction of the one.[42]

In the absence of the *Un*, comm-*un*-cation seems to be impossible. In different terms (or in terms of difference), a paralectic creates static by constantly practicing words that once seemed clear. *Le parasite* means not only animal or vegetable organism that lives at the expense of an other (called the host), carrying detriment to it, but without destroying it." It also means "disturbances in the reception of radio-electric signals. *Parasites which impede listening to an emission.*"[43]   Inasmuch as *le parasite* interferes with the emission and reception of messages (and of much else), the irreducibly paradoxical neuter faults the hermeneutical circle by interrupting interpretation. While hermeneutical conversation tries to heal the tear and wipe away the tear of the *Riss*, *l'entretien infini* of paralectics "affirms interruption and rupture."[44]   Within the paralogic of paralectics, the parasitic inter-play of dialogue and the discourse of the other issues in interruption, which, though unspeakable, makes speech possible. Neither inside nor outside, the *entre* of *l'entretien* is (impossibly) the condition of the possibility and the impossibility of communication.

In the first chapter ("Rats Meals") of the first part ("Interrupted Meals") of his book entitled *Le Parasite*, Michel Serres comments on the far-reaching implications of the conversation between two rats sitting on a Persian rug.

Someone once compared the undertaking of Descartes to the action of a man who sets his house on fire in order to hear the noise the rats make in the attic at night. These noises of running, scurrying, chewing, and gnawing that interrupt his sleep. I want to sleep peacefully. Good-bye then. To hell with the building that the rats come to ruin. I want to think without an error, communicate without a parasite.... But at night, the rats return to the foundation.... The rats come back. They are, as the saying goes, always already there. Part of

31

the building. The errors, trembling, confusion, obscurity are part of knowledge; noise is part of communication, part of the house.[45]

Rats, it seems, do make a difference. A difference that might be the rending *Riss* of *Unter-Schied*, a difference that is always different and an other that is forever other. Serres suggests, "Maybe the radical origin of things is really that difference or fault, even though classical rationalism damned it to hell. In the beginning was the noise."[46] This noisy "beginning" is no ordinary beginning but "is" a beginning that makes all ending impossible, a beginning that marks the impossibility of ending. As that which never ends, the "beginning" of the neuter is the "before" of play—the before that is forever "before the alternative of presence and absence." A dialogue that does not incorporate difference and appropriate the other by becoming dialectical must repeatedly "speak" the outlines of the between.

PATIENCE

The play of dialectical/hermeneutical conversation tends to be an impatient power play. In Serres' words: "Imperative of the purge. Thus exclude, the third, the Demon, prospopoeia of noise. If we want peace, if we desire an agreement between object and subject, the object appearing at the moment of the agreement, as the Last Supper as well as in the laboratory, in the dialogue as on the blackboard, we have to get together, assembling, reassembling, against whoever troubles our relations, the water of our channel. He is on the other bank [sometimes the Left, sometimes the West], the rival is. He is our common enemy. Our collective is the expulsion of the stranger, of the enemy, of the parasite. The laws of hospitality become the laws of hostility. Whatever the size of the group, from two on up to all humankind, the transcendental condition of its constitution is the existence of the Demon."[47] "The Demon"... "the demonized other" marks the return of the (repressed) rats.

When fully developed, hermeneutics tends to become culturally imperialistic. "The attempt to edify (ourselves or others)," Rorty maintains, "may consist in the hermeneutic activity of making connections between our own culture and some exotic culture or historical period, or between our own discipline and another discipline which seems to pursue incommensurable aims in an incommensurable vocabulary."[48] As I have stressed, the participants in dialectical/hermeneutical conversation move toward the other so they can return to themselves enriched. The "exotic" edifies only when it is first domesticated and then assimilated. The imperialistic implications of this strategy of interpretation become clear in a remarkable statement that Rorty makes in an essay entitled "Pragmatism, Relativism, Irrationalism." According to Rorty, the pragmatist "can only say, with Hegel, that truth and justice lie in the direction marked by the successive stages of *European* thought."[49] *Bildung*, it seems, is identified with the cultural tradition of the West. Other cultural traditions are valued only insofar as they aid Westerners "in becoming new beings."

Though not immediately apparent, this cultural imperialism grows out of the interpretation of the subject that emerges in modern European philosophy. As we have seen, Rorty credits Gadamer with rescuing "the romantic notion of man as self-creative" from the problematic metaphysical framework of nineteenth-century idealism. Hermeneutics, however, remains more metaphysical than most of its proponents are willing to admit. The self-creative subject, which receives comprehensive expression in Hegel's System, is essentially *constructive* and thus fundamentally impatient. In the final analysis, the im-patient subject finds difference or

33

otherness insufferable. The end of dialogue is monologue and, as Blanchot insists, monologue tends to be "imperious."[50]

While dialectic issues in a dialogue that is a monologue, paralectic interrupts monological discourse by allowing "impossibility" to be spoken.

> We have at first two important distinctions that correspond to a dialectical exigency and to a non-dialectical exigency of speech: the pause that permits exchange and the wait that measured infinite distance. But with waiting, it is not only the lofty rupture preparing the poetic act that affirms itself, but also, and at the same time, other forms of cessation, very profound, very perverse, more and more perverse, and always such that if one distinguishes them, the distinction does not avert, but rather postulates ambiguity. We have thus "distinguished" three forms: one where emptiness [*le vide*] makes itself work—the other where emptiness is fatigue, unhappiness—the other, the ultimate, the hyperbolic, where idleness [*désoeuvrement*] (perhaps thought) marks itself. To interrupt oneself in order to understand oneself/one another. To understand oneself/one another in order to speak. Finally, only speaking to interrupt oneself and to render possible the impossible interruption.[51]

Le partage des voix ... l'attente qui mesure la distance infini. L'attente: waiting, awaiting, expectation, hope ... Patience: *patior*, to suffer. The possibility of the im-possible (*in + possibilis* [*poti-*]) implies a certain im-potence (*in + potens* [*poti-*]). In the play of paralectics, the dialectical struggle for mastery gives way to the patient suffering of the unmasterable dis-course of the other. To respond to the other, one must learn to be patient, or, more accurately, one must learn how to allow patience to arrive.

34

The patient (subject) is always (already) passive before active. The suffering sub-ject receives itself as well as the other (sub-ject) from an other other that is the tear of dif-ference "itself."

Rats are not always demons. Sometimes the other for which the rat is a vehicle can be a god.

> Gajasura had obtained the privilege of not being killed by a beast, a man, a god, or a demon. Pulliar [Ganesa] not being one of these, as he was half god, half elephant, was the only one who could deal with him victoriously. The giant broke off the god's right tusk, but Pulliar, using it as a javelin, transfixed Gajamukha Gajasura, who transformed himself into a rat and became the vehicle of the god.[52]

As the keeper of the gate, "Ganesa is sometimes called Vighnesa or lord [isa] of obstacles [vighna]. The word vighna is itself a compound made up of the prefix vi, meaning away, asunder, and ghna, a term appearing in compound that means striking with, destroying, from the root han, strike, kill. A vighna can be anything that prevents, interrupts, diverts, or impedes anything else. It is any kind of resistance." Ganesa, whose vehicle is a rat, seems to be something like a parasite that is a pharmakon—not only Gift but also gift. "By enlisting Ganesa's aid, the devotee acknowledges the inevitability of obstruction, one's own limited powers of control over the destiny of the action, and the necessity of including the power inherent in the resistance—that is, Vighnesa, the deity residing within the obstacle—as an ally in the undertaking."[53]

To meet a rat that is other than the demonized other of the West, it might be necessary to travel East—from middle to far—in search of an East that "is" different ... different from a construction through which the West

35

converses with itself while pretending to listen to someone/something other.

NOTES

. A version of this essay is included in a forthcoming volume entitled *TEARS*, which ⁀ill be published by the State University of New York Press.

. Richard Rorty, *Consequences of Pragmatism*, pp. 103-04.

. *Ibid.*, p. 92.

. See, *inter alia*, M. H. Abrams, Natural Supernaturalism: Tradition and Revolution ₁ Romantic Literature, and Jean Hyppolite, Genesis and Structure of Hegel's henomenology, trans. S. Cherniak and J. Heckman (Evanston: Northwestern ⁀niversity Press, 1974).

. Richard Rorty, Philosophy and the Mirror of Nature (Princeton: Princeton ⁀niversity Press, 1979), p. 318.

. It is precisely Hegel's rejection of the notion of "edification" that leads ⁀ierkegaard to describe some of his own writings as "Edifying Discourses." See, ⁀difying Discourses, trans. David F. and Lillian M. Swenson (New York: Harper and ₒow, 1958).

. The etymology of the word "edify" underscores the close relationship between ⁀lification and building or construction. "Edify" derives from the Latin æficiare, ⁀des, ædis, dwelling + ficare, to make. The Danish word for "edify" is opbygge, op, ₁ + bygge, to build. Compare the German erbauen, build, raise, erect, construct; ⁀lify. Apparently opting for "accuracy" rather than elegance, the most recent ⁀anslators of Kierkegaard's writings insist on rendering Opbyggelige Taler as ⁀pbuilding Discourses."

Rorty, Philosophy and the Mirror of Nature, pp. 358-59.

Ibid., p. 359.

⁀). Hans-George Gadamer, Truth and Method (New York: Seabury Press, 1975), ⁀12. Quoted by Rorty, Philosophy and the Mirror of Nature, p. 362.

11. Rorty, <u>Philosophy and the Mirror of Nature</u>, p. 377. Rorty misleadingly cite Kierkegaard's <u>Concluding Unscientific Postscript</u> at this point. When read in th context of his overall argument, Kierkegaard's claim that "truth is subjectivity" cal: into question the kind of humanism that Gadamer and Rorty support.

12. Rorty, <u>Philosophy and the Mirror of Nature</u>, p. 360.

13. Hegel, <u>Phenomenology of Spirit</u>, p. 10. This passage calls for two addition comments. First, Hegel clearly indicates his low esteem for edification by his use « the verb <u>sinken</u>. Second, a phrase like "<u>ein Spielen der Liebe mit sich selbst</u>" mak« Derrida's discussion of the significance of Rousseau's preoccupation with masturbati« much more telling than many commentators are willing to admit. See, C Grammatology, especially pp. 141-164.

14. The recognition of the role played by Schiller and Kant in the genesis « hermeneutics is important for several reasons. In the first place, Schiller's <u>Lette</u> present a notion of <u>Bildung</u> that dominates later thinking. Second, Kant's use of tl notion of play in his account of the work of art exercises considerable influence « nineteenth- and twentieth-century aesthetic theory. As we shall see, Gadamer develo his views of play in the context of his discussion of the work of art. For a mo complete account of the importance of Schiller's notion of play for Hege philosophy; see: Mark C. Taylor, <u>Journeys to Selfhood: Hegel and Kierkegaard</u>, p 71-90.

15. Gadamer, <u>Truth and Method</u>, p. 97. Emphasis added.

16. <u>Ibid</u>., p. 97.

17. <u>Ibid</u>., p. 111.

18. <u>Ibid</u>., p. 111.

19. <u>Ibid</u>., pp. 113-14.

20. <u>Ibid</u>., p. 341. In this passage, Gadamer is concerned with dialogue partners w are contemporaries. As the following text makes clear, the implications conversation are the same when the discussion partner is in the "past." "Ev« encounter with tradition that takes place within historical consciousness involves «

38

•erience of the tension between text and the present. The hermeneutic task consists not covering up this tension by attempting a naive assimilation but consciously ำging it out. This is why it is part of the hermeneutic approach to project an :orical horizon that is different from the horizon of the present. Historical ·sciousness is aware of its own otherness and hence distinguishes the horizon of ■ition from its own. On the other hand, it is itself, as we are trying to show, only ำething laid over a continuing tradition, and hence it immediately recombines what as distinguished in order, in the unity of the historical horizon that it thus acquires, ำecome again one with itself" (p. 273).

This is not, of course, to imply that Gadamer and Rorty agree about everything. ， obvious that they differ on a variety of relevant details. I would insist, however, they concur on most of the basic points in their theories of interpretation.

Jacques Derrida, Writing and Difference, p. 292.

Rorty, Consequences of Pragmatism, p. 92.

Ibid., p. 140.

Ibid., pp. 94-95.

Derrida, Writing and Difference, p. 292. Another way to approach Rorty's ำrision of Derrida is to examine his understanding of presence and absence. ·ing failed to recognize the difference between Gadamer's and Derrida's views of ·, Rorty tends to regard absence as the absence of presence, which is the presence ำsence. What Rorty has not thought is that which "must be conceived before the ำnative of presence and absence." In hermeneutical terms, the presence of the nce of the represented object creates the possibility of self-presence of the ำsenting subject. To think that which is neither present nor absent is to think the ำssibility of presence as such.

Ibid., p. 293.

Maurice Blanchot, Le pas au-de là, p. 158.

Ibid., p. 293.

30. Jean-Luc Nancy, Le Partage des Voix (Paris: Gailée, 1982), p. 86.

31. Heidegger, "Language," Poetry, Language, Thought, pp. 206-07. Those wl espouse hermeneutics frequently cite the first sentence in this quotation. They usua do not recognize the difficulties that the notion of difference suggested in the rest the text pose for the hermeneutical reading of language. For a more extens consideration of Heidegger's position, see above, chapter eleven.

32. One of Nancy's chief concerns in Le Partage des Voix is to show how the not of the Riss necessitates a reinterpretation of Heidegger's hermeneutical circle.

33. Nancy, Le Partage des Voix, pp. 86-87.

34. Ibid., p. 88.

35. The use of the word "converse" in this context might be misleading. That wh struggles toward articulation in Blanchot's entretien is not simply the opposite of Hegelian dialectic and hermeneutical conversation but is that which both breaks v and makes possible the structure of opposition itself.

36. This is the title of the first section of L'Entretien Infini.

37. Blanchot, L'Entretien Infini, pp. 107-08.

38. Recall Derrida's claim in "Structure, Sign and Play": "Play is the disruptior presence. The presence of an element is always a signifying and substitutive refere inscribed in a system of differences and the movements of a chain. Play is alw play of absence and presence, but if it is to be thought radically, play must conceived of before the alternative of presence and absence." See above, note 2

39. Blanchot, L'Entretien Infini, p. 91.

40. Ibid., p. 99.

41. Blanchot, Le pas au-delà, p. 97.

42. Blanchot, Le pas au-delà, p. 97.

43. Le Petit Robert, Dictionnaire de la Langue Française.

Blanchot, L'Entretien Infini, p. 116.

Michel Serres, The Parasite, trans. L.R. Schehr (Baltimore: Johns Hopkins iversity Press, 1982), p. 12. In view of the importance of negation for the problem interruption, it is interesting to note that the French word for "meal," repas, can be written: re-pas.

Ibid., p. 13.

Ibid., p. 56.

Rorty, Philosophy and the Mirror of Nature, p. 360.

Rorty, Consequences of Pragmatism, p. 173. Emphasis added.

In a para-enthetical aside, Blanchot writes: "Let us recall the terrible monologues Hitler and of every Chief of State. He enjoyed being alone to speak and, enjoying haughty solitary speech, imposed it on others, without constraint, as a superior and reme speech. He participated in the same violence of the dictare--the repetition of imperious monologue" (L'Entretien Infini, pp. 106-07).

Blanchot, L'Entretien Infini, p. 112.

Quoted in Paul B. Courtright, Ganesa: Lord of Obstacles, Lord of Beginnings w York: Oxford University Press, 1985), p. 80.

Ibid., pp. 156-57.

III
DIF/FERENCE AND ITS
DISGUISES

ROY WAGNER
PROFESSOR OF ANTHROPOLOGY
UNIVERSITY OF VIRGINIA

Just what sort of discipline is anthropological fieldwork, if the fieldworker, never really "in" his or her native culture nor in that of the research subjects, is hardly "between" them either? To imagine any of these possibilities we would have to imagine the fieldworker as an analogy rather than a person. And so we must perforce imagine "culture" to be analogical in nature instead, a kind of comparison or assumption the fieldworker is forced to make: that these people are not mad, and I am not mad, and therefore analogies must be possible that would render each comprehensible in the relative terms of the other.

But the relative terms of the fieldworker under normal field conditions are those of dislocation and distraction: differentiation has already been accomplished and the "other" is scarcely necessary to it. The anthropologist is an outsider cast among insiders, a differential, not simply of culture or condition alone, but of cultural condition. What happens then is that analogies are drawn up that conceal absence behind presence, difference within similarity. The fieldworker may be adopted into a lineage, as happened to me on one occasion; in another instance a Daribi[1] friend observed that I was like a brother-in-law, a relative by marriage.

This was no mere courtesy, for a Daribi marriage is also fundamentally difference made over, a bride made out of personal or familial rather than cultural context, and one makes over the difference by drawing analogies of relationship with her family. Should she bear children, these too are marked by her difference, and wealth must be passed from her husband to her natal family to redeem this difference from the woman's father and brothers, who are their "owners." Since all Daribi are born and redeemed in this way, a case can be made for my friend's analogy as being the root analogy of Daribi relationship at large. And it bears a family resemblance as well with the analogic praxis of "culture" in the field, with its redeeming of difference.

But we must be careful, for this is only an analogy, one in which ownership or propriety is defined by conditional or contextual difference. A developed strain of analogy, in other words, such as the Daribi people of interior New Guinea present as their myth of human life and relationship, or the anthropologist must perforce create as a way out of an existential and intellectual dilemma, can never make difference go away. It transforms difference, visits that of the mother upon the child, re-imagines it as the reciprocal and inverse subject of its attempts to overcome it. Thus an analogy of relatedness makes a merely analogic difference as its shadow, makes a Daribi woman's childhood and upbringing, her natality, the "owner" of her children's, makes the fieldworker's alienation from home and surroundings, becomes the difference that haunts the analogy of another way of life as a "culture."

The analogical or relative mode, which is likely the only one in which culture can be understood, delineated, or realized, is incapable of forming absolute identities as it is of generating complete differentiation. What it produces are "bound" forms in which analogic (metaphoric or metonymic) similarities or linkages acquire their significance solely by contrast with properly corresponding differences, and vice versa. Difference and similarity, in other words, form a sort of contrast that opposes a positive photographic print to its negative transparency. A Daribi child is then redeemed by payments from a "difference" resulting from its mother's differentiation from her own family, but that

43

differentiation is in turn significant only because payments are necessary to redeem it.

Cultural comparison and similarity, "knowing" another culture insofar as an intimate acquaintance and participation are required for it, is likewise imprinted with the self-differentiation of the "knower" from his or her own tradition. And this also means that estrangement from one's own tradition is entirely derivative of and relative to the analogic sense one makes of the other. An "unbound" difference, one with no analogic shadow to point up the significance of its differentiation, may well be possible in the anthropological context, but it would be very difficult to determine what it might mean.

Ethnography does not, then, describe "culture" as it may be for those born and raised to it, for there is no difference to separate such people from their own conventions and thus form a basis for totalizing them analogically. *Their* bound forms are constructed within the frameworks of custom and language. Culture is always described from the "outside" as it never could have existed for its members or insiders, and the analogies by which we get to it are always reflexive "unpictures" of the conventions one began with. I had always hoped to be flattered by the special attention and recognition that indigenous subjects gave to my spoken and written analyses of their usages, especially their uncritical fascination (for there are Daribi people who read English) with idiomatic nicety. But in looking for some sort of approbation for my ideas I had entirely missed the point. They were not interested in my thoughts but my words, not so much impressed with what I was able to comprehend as with what of it I was able to put into words — a remarkable gratuitous body skill, rather like riding a monocycle.

Analogy minus imprinted difference is just words. One needs the analogic of "culture" only when difference becomes relevant. Hence it is that the classics of early ethnographers are so often consulted by postcolonial "subjects" seeking to resurrect their ancient rites—what they are seeking is precisely the shape of their difference from the culture that has overwhelmed them.

In some despair of bringing philosophy to the aid of philosophy, I have begun my comments on Mark Taylor's fine evocation of Heidegger's *Unter/schied* deliberately with a subject I know well enough to despair of. A difference bound to the analogy that brings it into relief is not dif-ference in Taylor's sense. Reading back from my examples to Heidegger's language enabling dif-ference, every linguistic difference or distinction reflects in some measure the radical differentiation between subject and its expression or predication. Since the caesura is not complete, the subject remains bound as a linguistic subject to its predicate, and the ontological differentiation is masked by the superficial intentionality of speech. This is the ground of analogy, the interpretive matrix where subject is expected in the shape of a message, a predication, something to say of it.

Language, and the whole suspension of dif-ference that we call "discourse," is then a disqualifying of the Riss or tear between subject and predication. As an enabling pretense of being able to represent what its exchange among speakers is not, language substitutes word or syntax for person, thing, intention, condition, aspect — stakes its very reason for existence on the representation of differentiation and similarity, or contiguity, within the same medium. To achieve even a minimal differentiation in the context provided by such a medium, one would have to differentiate against the medium itself, something that a verbal trope does, in fact, do.

To the extent that such a trope is *not* understood, interpreted, theorized as a differentiation *against* the conventional expectations of a language, it becomes readable as an iconic "sign," something that uses language in a provocative way to form the possibility of an image, to "redescribe" (as if conventional language described) in Paul Ricoeur's terms. Interpretation or redescription is the facility enabled, or required, by the treatment of trope in semiotic terms, as a kind of language use. We assume in other words a grounding in the conventionality of language, and then *react* to the disturbance or differentiation made in that conventional expectation, calling our reaction an icon or an image. Such a reaction and the "sign" that it makes of difference is already an interpretation of itself when we decide to approach it semiotically.

But if we were to look to the effect of the trope as just simply difference, the bare impact or disjunction of lexical items without considering its "meaning," we would discover its own self-demonstration as to how it is to be interpreted. Every trope is in this sense a "performative," an event that describes its own enactment as it enacts its description. The fact of differentiation is then a self-sign of non-linguistic value whose reverberations across the scales of language are no more than overtones or aftershocks. The real echo or counter-stroke to a differentiating percept is not a reaction but an action — *another* difference made in deference to its self-demonstrating message. (An example would be the order of play in a chess game, where the move that follows another is not an interpretive reaction but a counting difference.) It would seem that dif/ference only becomes recognizable when its self-injunction is brought to realization in this way.

Dif/ference is then self-enacting or holographic difference, the widening or chain-reactive crack that eventually faults the medium itself, as move and countermove lead ultimately to the checkmate that breaks the setting of the game. Insofar as the checkmate that ends it is the object or intent of a game of chess, every move that is *not* checkmate "binds" itself to the chain of previous and subsequent moves in a suspension of "game" toward the anticipation of its closure.

One could say that play hazards the legitimation of its concept, and "recovers" that legitimacy when its setting has been brought to an allowable conclusion. The legitimacy of the "score" is then conferred upon the winner. Though tempers may be raised, egos bruised, the win or loss is, we are reminded, nonetheless bound and bounded by the legitimacy of the game. A Grand Master who won every game he or she had ever played would not, in this mode of thinking, be distinguished *as against* the game, would not have won a match *against* chess, but necessarily *through* it, through the legitimacy that binds checkmate victories to the rules for checkmate. Hence breaking the setting of the game is understood to make its difference *out*side of the confines of its rules, or among the players, perhaps in a game called "life."

A game like chess breaks its setting in order to recover its legitimacy as a game, as a doorbell buzzer breaks its own circuit in order to do the job of buzzing. Both bind their necessary difference to their settings so that the effect of a difference is made outside of those settings. An unstructured play situation, where the rules may be uncertain or developed on an *ad hoc* basis as the play proceeds, hazards its rules rather than its difference, like those Melanesian soccer matches that are played until the score is even. The alternative is an uncounted or unbound difference, the difference of the game becoming unconfined difference in the world, the game played "for real" (a situation that has been known to occur when those Melanesian soccer matches that are played until the score is even.)

If the Grand Master never wins his final tournament against the game itself, the doorbell almost never breaks its mechanism in lieu of its circuit, the word has yet to be spoken that will break language of its repetitive habit, this tells us something about what is hazarded in cultural and language games and why. Without the hazard of dif-ference there would be nothing to lose, and therefore nothing to gain. Like the Hegelian

47

"subject," dif-ference must be there, but also as in that case it must be deflected.

But if we should want to imagine "culture," simply for the sake of illustration, as the game or set of rules that language is often imagined to be, then this at least suggests the possibility of a self-conscious "outsider" like the anthropologist assuming the role of the Grand Master taking on the game itself as an opponent. It is a dif-ference among "games" that is hazarded, rather than the rules of one of them, or least it is the difference that other rules make to one's own. And so long as what we call cultural difference is not difference, a tear in the fabric of humanity, the unstructured play of anthropology must locate the rules or analogies that bind that difference.

It is for this reason that anthropology, as it is practiced, taught, written about, is not a paralectic as Mark Taylor speaks of it, why it does not come up with answers to match the scale of its naive and original questions. The admission of a cultural difference that could not be bridged by analogy, a cultural dif/ference, would deny the possibility of a theoretical solution. But that does not by any means deny the possibility of paralectic. People doubtless from time to time witness things that they cannot account for, particularly in unfamiliar or culturally estranged circumstances, yet discourse even on such a topic turns dif/ference back into difference merely to speak of it or think it.

It is quite possible, in view of that fact, that what we speak of as the differences between cultures are truly tears in the fabric of humanity, that the anthropological fieldworker is often in the position of the Grand Master taking on the game rather than the opponent. If the forms of language and thought compel the binding of differences to analogies as a condition of the effectiveness, might not dif/ference be in fact the *definitive* form of fieldwork experience? Is it not simply this that makes anthropological theories and descriptions so dissimilar to one another, even when the same

48

people or community is considered? A dif/ference in the rules of the game, in one's means of expression or description cannot be played according to those rules, described through those means. This is a problem, one of "... expressing what cannot be thought of, in view of thought's subjugation to essences" that, according to Victor Turner, "... has engaged the passionate attention of the ritual man in all places and ages."[1]

But of course ritual epitomizes what some are disposed to call the rules of a culture, and Turner's evocation of what is quintessential to culture itself as a performance of "what cannot be thought ..." makes a neat focal parallax, a binocular vision pulling the gulfs between cultures and the dif/ference within them into a kind of three-dimensional unity. To say that what is essential to a culture is a projection of the difference among cultures, or that cultures are only differentiable at all on the basis of like differences existing within them, would be to describe the outside parameters or facies of this unity. Its terms of performing the differences among cultures *as* culture, or realizing *a* culture as the differentiation necessary to perceiving "otherness," makes each of these the analogy of the other, the difference of each being bound into the analogic resolution of the other. This point might give us a more tangible explanation than "the force of tradition" to explain why Latin was the language both of the high mass and of scholarship in the Middle Ages, or why the Daribi simply use the designation of a nearby language group for the cryptic metaphors of their ritual songs, or call analogic language "*kewa*," "foreign" talk, "it's Greek to me."

If the necessary locking or binding of difference to analogy in this way, such that each is the contingency of the other, makes what could be called the language of the thinkable or sayable, then the sayable or thinkable, as Turner's comments indicate, amounts to a kind of necessary surrogate for dif/ference. And if the world's substances and objectivities, its social relationships in commonsense as well as anthropological terms, could not be located or dealt with without that surrogate, that makes the whole world of bound differences, of tangibles, sayables, do-ables, the outside surface of a necessarily central and necessarily invisible core of dif/ference. To speak language is to pretend that dif/ference is linguistic differentiation, to imagine it as a differing of subject and object, or of tense, aspect, mood, of kind or intention. To use number is to code dif/ference in terms of quantitative or functional difference, and devices like the computer facilitate the mimicry of a human perceptual difference through the on/off switching of current.

In this sense dif/ference is simply the unimaginable limit of all the forms of discrimination we know, the epitomizing form not only of what human beings project upon the world but also of *how* they should do so. But in the same sense it is also philosophically baffling in that it presents no ground of commonality against which an alterity may be projected, as for instance gender difference is bound by the underlying analogic of species, or red/green by that of color. It is not, so to speak, the *difference* among differences, setting them into a relation of alterity to one another, but their *similarity*, that which they all share in common.

Every instance of difference we might be able to identify, whether linguistic—lexical, grammatical, syntactic, generally perceptual (observational/experiential), or within or among cultural forms, is then an instantiation of the dif/ference that all discriminations share in common. Each manifestation of the common form might be regarded as a scalar projection, a sort of magnification or diminution by virtue of imagined analogy and hence a change in analogic "scale," of the common ground of Heidegger's Riss. Since we fasten upon an imagined analogy in every case as the vehicle of "meaning" connecting the differentiated terms, it follows that meaning or understanding is itself the factor that obliterates any possible awareness of dif/ference as a totalizing phenomenon. In other words, meaning or understanding in its accessible cultural or linguistic

50

forms is wedded to scale-change, or what might be called the difference among differences, rather than their similarity or common ground.

In its received form of "knowledge," differentiation within language or culture as well as differentiation among cultures, then, understanding is a matter of scale-change, an assimilation of dif/ference to the analogic means of sorting it. Dif/ference might then be defined for our purposes as differentiation that "keeps its scale" in all of its instantiations, and therefore as a kind of holography behind the scenes of thought. As a speculative exercise, it could be thought of as a crack or a flaw running down through all the scales of cultural meaning, one that necessarily presents itself as the same fragmentation or fractability at every point. One might call it the "crack between the worlds," or, understood holographically, the "Indra-net" of Hindu cosmology.

The constructionist thought that is the stock-in-trade of academic discourse bases itself on what Bateson has called "the difference that makes a difference,"[2] the differences, that is, among differences, or part-whole relations. Interpretation as well as the individual/collective of the social sciences, statecraft, and jurisprudence, makes up its analogies on the basis of a necessary *relation* between part and whole, the whole being equal to the sum of its parts, or perhaps greater than such a sum. But the self-scaling of dif/ference transforms that relation into an *identity*, wherein whole and part are intrinsically equal to one another, an identity that effectively precludes analogy or relation. In other words, analogy and the meanings it elicits, as well as any understanding founded upon differentiation *not* being self-scaling, or holographic.

Put in simple terms, this means that it would not only be pointless or unnecessary to seek an overarching analogic to which dif/ference could be bound, but in fact impossible to find one. For the self-scaling of dif/ference is at once its own differentiation and its own analogy, as the difference that all differentiation shares in common — at once subject and

51

ROY WAGNER

object. It is the "zero," or better, the "ground zero," of understanding. But then, zero for zero, it is also true that the discovery of the zero (credited to the Hindus, as well as the Meso-Americans) marks the *beginning*, rather than the end, of sophisticated mathematical thinking.

REFERENCES

1. Victor Turner, *Revelation and Divination in Ndembu Ritual.* Ithaca: Cornell University Press, 1975; p. 187.

2. Gregory Bateson, *Steps to an Ecology of Mind*, New York: Ballantine Books, 1972; p. 381.

IV
THE POLITICS OF DIFFERENCE

M.E. BRINT

PROFESSOR OF POLITICAL THEORY
UNIVERSITY OF VIRGINIA

WITH DAVID HENNIGAN, WILLIAM WEAVER,
AND ANDREW WICKS

The history of society and culture is, in large measure, a history of the struggle with the endlessly complex problems of difference and otherness. Never have the questions posed by difference and otherness been more pressing than they are today. For an era dominated by the struggle between among, and against various "isms" — communism, fascism, totalitarianism, capitalism, racisim, sexism, etc. — the issue of difference is undeniably political. Is difference tolerable? Are others to be encouraged to express and cultivate their differences? Or is difference intolerable? Are others who are different to be converted, integrated, dominated, excluded, or repressed?[1]

With this passage, Mark Taylor opens what he calls the "Encore" to his most recent book, *Altarity*. No doubt, Taylor is quite right in suggesting "the undeniably political urgency of the issue of difference." To offer an obvious example, the voices of women have too often been silenced, submerged, and forced to enter what Mr. Taylor might call the realm of the Other: the region silently stretching beyond the circumference of "normal" discursive practice and acknowledged ethical meaning. In general, this systematic exclusion of the significance of difference no doubt results in a politics of appropriation and domination.

In what follows, I will examine some of the implications of Taylor's remarks regarding the politics of difference. I will begin with a dramaturgical reading of Hegel's "comic" approach to the "tragic" problem of difference. In concert with both Taylor and Rorty, I will suggest the way in which Hegel's resolution to this problem is articulated in his language of the Absolute. In "thinking beyond comedy," I will turn to a critical assessment of the respective approaches to the politics of difference offered by both Taylor and Rorty.

THE DIALECTICS OF COMEDY

In the works of G.W.F. Hegel, the comic tradition of western political and philosophical thought undoubtedly reaches its zenith.[2] Like Dante's Divine Comedy, Hegel offers us a daring philosophical odyssey predicated on the principles of unity, harmony and synchronicity. In contrast to Dante's more personal pilgrimage to the universal, however, Hegel's journey encompasses and comprises nothing less than the spiritual odyssey of all of reality itself.[3] In his work, we are presented with the journey of Geist [Spirit/Mind] as it comes to know itself in determinate reality.

Propelled by a narrative of inner contradiction, the dialectical logic of Spirit's odyssey is reflected in Hegel's definition of classical tragedy. Indeed, recall Hegel's claim that there are three fundamental movements inherent in the narrative structure of classical tragedy. First, he tells us, we find the existence of two ethical forces pervading the landscape. Next, these forces are set in opposition to one another. When taken independently, Hegel claimed, these opposing forces are equally justifiable

THE POLITICS OF DIFFERENCE

(ii 1196). However, as A.C. Bradley put it, the tragic fact is that they are also ultimately incompatible.

> It will be agreed that in all tragedy there is some sort of conflict — conflict of feelings, modes of thought, desires, wills, purposes; conflict of persons with one another, or with circumstances, or with themselves; one, several, or all of these kinds of conflict as the case may be .... The essentially tragic fact is the self-division and intestinal warfare of the ethical substance, not so much the war of good with evil as the war of good with good.[4]

In this passage, taken from his influential lecture on Hegel's aesthetics, Bradley no doubt demonstrates a remarkable sensitivity to the structure and character of tragic conflict. Nevertheless, he implicitly assumes the existence of an identifiable "ethical substance" in virtue of which opposing moral claims find their essential unity. In this way, he correctly follows Hegel's vision of the "comic" resolution necessary to all tragedy.

"Whatever may be the necessity of the tragic collision," Hegel tells us, "it is no less a claim that is asserted by the resolution of this division" (ii 1209). In his theory, Hegel may thus be seen as offering a conception of tragedy as implicit comedy. Indeed, as Northrop Frye reminds us, such comic appropriation of the landscape of tragedy is not uncommon in literary history: "As for the conception of tragedy as implicit comedy, we may notice how often tragedy closes on the major chord of comedy: the Aeschylean trilogy, for instance, proceed to what is really a comic resolution, and so do many tragedies of Euripides."[5] Through such appropriation, comedy not only seems to follow tragedy, but, in Walter Kerr's words, "appears to derive inexorably from its spirit."[6]

55

However noble its goal, rich its theoretical material and daring its historical conjugations, Hegel's appropriation and resolution of ethical conflict is predicated on various schemes of value subordination and conversion. Subordination eliminates moral conflict through the creation of hierarchy while conversion transforms values through their subsumption into yet new principles of unity. Appropriation is thus achieved through the devaluation of the significance of moral differences. Martha Nussbaum has made this point rather succinctly: "To do justice to the nature or identity of two distinct values," she tells us,

> requires doing justice to their difference; and doing justice to their difference — both their qualitative distinctness and their numerical separateness — requires seeing that there are, at least potentially, circumstances in which the two will collide. Distinctness requires articulation from, bounding-off against. This, in turn, entails the possibility of opposition — and for the agent who is committed to both — of conflict.[7]

No doubt, Hegel's attempt to eliminate such conflict rests on the fundamental commensurability of the values at issue. But, as Nussbaum implies, if such commensurability can be achieved only by devaluing difference, then Hegel's schemes of appropriation are certainly unwarranted.

In this way, Hegel's comic achievement is subject to the danger inherent in all such moral absolutizing. As Milan Kundera ironically suggests in his *Book of Laughter and Forgetting*:

> People have always aspired to an idyll, a garden where nightingales sing, a realm of harmony where the world does not rise up as a stranger against man nor man against other

men, where the world and all its people are molded from a
single stock and the fire lighting up the heavens is the fire
burning in the hearts of men, where everyman is a note in a
magnificent Bach fugue and anyone who refuses his note is
a mere black dot, useless and meaningless, easily caught and
squashed between the fingers like an insect.[8]

In Kundera's terms, the deep pleasure of ethical totality is echoed in the
"serious laughter of the angels" who eternally express their unity and joy
of being (233). Yet, this divine laughter and joy, he insists, when carried
to extremes, denotes the "enthusiastic laughter of angel-fanatics, who are
so convinced of their world's significance that they are ready to hang
anyone not sharing their joy" (233). Echoing with such divine laughter, the
tradition of western political theory has no doubt experienced its problem
with angels.

THINKING BEYOND COMEDY

Mark Taylor's Satire

In thinking beyond Hegel's logic of the Absolute, Mark Taylor has
offered what might be dramaturgically described as a Satirical response.
Parasitic upon comic resolution, his satire acts to disrupt the promise of a
happy ending by rupturing the transparency of linguistic exchange that
comedy seeks to establish. Taylor's narrative achieves such disruption
through parody. It seeks, he says, to mime the uncommunicable Other. As
Hayden White suggests, such "satire gains its effect precisely by frustrating
normal expectations about the kinds of [endings] provided by ... Romance,
Comedy, or Tragedy, as the case may be."[9]

57

Indeed, rejecting the resolutive aspect of Hegel's comic double negation, Taylor's satire also rejects the "tragic" "anti-dialectical logic of either/or."[10] In this respect, he seems to be playing Hegel off Kierkegaard. For Taylor, Kierkegaard's wholly/Holy other stands outside the grasp of the Hegelian system's claim that every "other" is a negation of itself; something that can be brought back within the presence of itself. In Taylor's view, the "wholly/Holy" other must always be, for us, something "mythical" or "mystical." The only thing we can say about the "other" is that we can't grasp it: the "other" is, in Mr. Taylor's words, the "unspeakable."

By advocating what he calls the "paralogic" of "the neither both/and nor either/or," Taylor outlines the domain of the "between."

> The "between" (l'entre-deux), which is neither positive nor negative, neither is nor is not, is a difference or an other that cannot be dialectically sublated through the duplicitous positivity of double negation (p.29).

For Taylor, paralectics "simultaneously creates the space for dialogue and neutralizes the transparency of the signs exchanged" (p.30). In other words, it is a dialogue which constantly disrupts, interrupts and ruptures itself at every pause. Against Hegel's appropriative schemes, Taylor thus poses the ineffable other as that which neither yearns for nor yields to, but satirically ruptures dialectical sublation.

In a similar fashion, he pits this other against what he takes to be Rorty's Hegelian-hermeneutical approach. He writes:

> Over against Hegel, Rorty insists that the final chapter of the story cannot be written and thus a conclusive end is forever delayed. The deferral of absolute knowledge creates the

possibility of an unending conversation that is *essentially hermeneutical*. From this point of view, hermeneutics can be understood as something like Hegelianism without absolute knowledge (p.15).

Calling Rorty's work, "essentially" hermeneutical, is certainly a curious way to describe either hermeneutics or Rorty's own anti-essentialist views. But, Rorty refuses to play the role of Gadamer in Taylor's satire. He is not advocating the "quest for certainty which never arrives." In fact, it is the very idea that we can create, discover, search or research for such certainty that Rorty is dropping.

More importantly, he is dropping the idea that language speaks us in an endlessly rupturing dialogue with the "Other." Indeed, if one takes the pragmatic turn in language with Rorty, then Taylor's paralectics begin to sound a bit like Wittgenstein's famous grunt. When Taylor claims that "a paralectic parodies a dialectic by miming the communication of that which is 'incommunicable," we are faced with the "unnameable proclaiming itself"; a border is thrown up between the thinkable and the unthinkable, between the sayable and the unsayable. But, how can the incommunicable be communicatively mimed? How might the unknowable, the unspeakable, be mimed? Wittgenstein tells us that when we come upon that which is unsayable we are inclined to utter an inarticulate grunt. Surely Taylor does not mean to imply that paralectic miming and Wittgensteinian grunting are the same thing. Of course, following Rorty's pragmatism, the point is that rather than feeling obliged to find the linguistic experience either profane or sacred, when we run up against "the between" of "the neither/nor," it might be more useful to ask how we got there and, more importantly, how can we improvise to get out?

Further, if like Rorty, one does not put much faith in the language of "presence," "representation," and "transparency," then one need not feel particularly threatened by a paralectics that "create static by constantly parasitizing words that once seemed clear." Indeed, if one accepts the contingency of language, as Rorty does, then one also might not feel frightened of finding rats chewing away at our linguistic foundations. Rather than seeing language as foundational, Rorty aligns himself with Wittgenstein's metaphor of alternative vocabularies as alternative tools that human beings use.[11] Recall that it was also Wittgenstein who likened language to an ancient village with different houses gradually added on to others, none of which bear a necessary relation to any other others, unless one thinks of the obvious relation they share -- humans use them. We expect ancient villages to have "rats" - it's hard to imagine one without them. If confronted by a rat, we try to find a way around it." As parasitic on the "language of transparency," however, Taylor's rats may be b(eat)ing a dead horse; both flogging and consuming that idea of linguistic transparency which is momentarily resurrected only to once again be destroyed in an endless play of difference.

So far, a good deal of emphasis has been placed on some of the problems with Taylor's reading of Rorty. What has not yet been addressed, however, is what I take to be the central "political" complaint Taylor lodges against Rorty. In Taylor's view, like the practitioners of hermeneutics, Rorty appears committed to an ethnocentric philosophy that is repressive of difference (pp.22,33). By way of conclusion, I will turn to Rorty's narrative and Taylor's complaint.

Rorty's American Romance

If Taylor offers us a satirical narrative of difference, in thinking beyond Hegel's comedy, Rorty seems to offer us a romance.

While in the past, Rorty has called himself a "tragic liberal," he has nevertheless consistently endorsed utopian enterprises aimed at expanding one's political imagination through romantic visions of future greatness. "To imagine great things is to imagine a great future for a particular community, a community one knows well, identifies with, can make plausible predictions about. In the modern world, this usually means one's nation. Political romance is, therefore, for the foreseeable future, going to consist of psalms of national future, rather than of the future of mankind."[12] While this idea may seem to substantiate Taylor's claims regarding Rorty's ethnocentrism, it should be noted that in his remarks, Rorty is referring to the national future of Brazil, not America.

However, in his most recent book, *Contingency, Irony and Solidarity*, Rorty may be closer to offering just such an American Romance; one that dissolves or evades (rather than appropriates) the problems of the past by "cashing in" on the liberal hopes of the future. His psalm to the future is undoubtedly cast in the ironic mode insofar as it takes the shape of a liberal utopia that stresses its own historical contingency. Indeed, he uses the term "ironist"

> to name the sort of person who faces up to the contingency of
> his or her own most central beliefs and desires .... Liberal
> ironists are people who include among these ungroundable
> desires their own hope that suffering will be diminished, that
> the humiliation of human beings by other human beings may
> cease (xv).

For Rorty, neither the comic dreams of communitarian politics nor the equally comic hopes of metaphysicians can offer a foundation or grounding for human solidarity. Rather, it is by becoming more sensitive to the often subtle forms of human cruelty that we expand and experience such

61

solidarity. For instance, literary works like those by Nabokov and Orwell often warn us against the insidious "tendencies to cruelty inherent in searches for autonomy" (144).

By autonomy, Rorty means the kind of thing which self-creating ironists like Nietzsche, Sartre, or Foucault seek (65). Rather than either ignoring or politicizing such attempts at radical self-creation or self-perfection, however, Rorty advocates privitizing autonomy. "Privitize the Nietzschean-Sartrean-Foucauldian attempt at authenticity and purity," he tells us, "in order to prevent yourself from slipping into a political attitude which will lead you to think that there is some social goal more important than avoiding cruelty" (65).

Publically and politically, Rorty endorses the institutions of contemporary liberal society that attempt to balance the preservation of individual liberty with the prevention of human suffering. "Indeed," in what must be read with a good deal of irony, Rorty tells us, "my hunch is that Western social and political thought may have had the *last* conceptual *revolution* it needs. J.S. Mill's suggestion that governments devote themselves to optimizing the balance between leaving people's private lives alone and preventing suffering seems to me pretty much the last word" (63). Indeed, as "humanity's most precious achievement," Rorty exclaims, "Nothing is more important" than protecting "these liberal institutions" against "thugs and theorists" alike.[13]

While there is much to be said on behalf of his liberal ideal, I do have some reservations about Rorty's "romance." First, I'm not sure whether Rorty's arguments about essentialism and anti-essentialism make "any difference or all of the difference." Indeed, for Rorty, calling a work "metaphysical" or "essentialist" seems to be something of an empty insult. If one thinks that a narrative couched in "metaphysical" terms is "true" (in the Jamesian sense), then one can just strip it of its metaphysical language through redescription. If one does not believe such a narrative is "true,"

THE POLITICS OF DIFFERENCE

then one can call it "metaphysical" and essentially drop it. But, "by definition," a distinction between texts one thinks are good in the way of belief and those which one thinks are not good in the way of belief, has nothing to do with whether or not such texts are "metaphysical."

To cite an obvious example, even though John Stuart Mill has the last word in his romance, Rorty's utopian politics are nevertheless drawn from the bete noir of anti-metaphysical thinking, Immanual Kant. Just as John Rawls has shed Kant's metaphysical trappings by canceling the "idea of a transhistorical" "absolutely valid" set of concepts which would serve as "philosophical foundations" of liberalism, Rorty identifies his own pragmatic romance with the "self-fulfilling triumph of the Enlightenment" (57).

Indeed, from Rorty's narrative perspective, a non-metaphysical, non-foundational, self-canceling, and contingent reading of Kant's *Metaphysical Elements of Justice*, would almost certainly amount to a pragmatic redescription of Rawls' first principle. Recall Kant's "Universal Principle of Justice": "I ought to act in such a way that my freedom can co-exist with the freedom of every other." While justifying this claim for freedom in terms of our historically contingent beliefs, both Rawls and Rorty undoubtedly endorse the fulfillment of Kant's liberal project. Moreover, by de-scientizing and de-philosophizing his enlightened thought, Kant's liberalism no doubt converges with that of Isaiah Berlin and J.S. Mill. In this way, while Kant may have lead philosophy departments astray for the last two hundred years, it seems that Rorty has not strayed too far from an updated American version of Kant's utopian ideal of liberalism.

As an American Romance, Rorty employs metaphors that are undoubtedly part of our dominant cultural vocabulary. For instance, he tells us that the American tradition of pragmatic thought allows us to "cash in" on our ideas. Rather than advocating "wholesale" constraints on conversation, Rorty appeals to what he calls, "the retail reasons which have brought one to one's present view."[14] In this way, as Christopher Norris has pointed out, "akin to current economists' parlance," Rorty uses the word "liberal" to describe "a kind of intellectual free-market outlook which wants to have done with all restrictive or legtimating checks and controls."[15]

While Rorty pays little or no attention to economic analysis in constructing his liberal utopia, one must question his use of this dominant metaphor insofar as it has a tendency to play a monopolistic role in his narrative. Don't get me wrong. The metaphor of exchange is certainly appropriate to describe the dominant discursive activities in one important sphere of our cultural practice, the sphere Rorty happens to ignore. But, surely a wholesale distribution of this metaphor is inappropriate given the complexity and plurality of our cultural practices.

Of course, in defense of Rorty, it might be claimed that the economic metaphor of the "market-place of ideas" is as old as Socrates. But, to my mind at least, such a claim is a bit like McDonald's using Bertolt Brecht's "Mac the Knife" as its theme song to sell hamburgers.[16] While Socrates' point was that the market is no place for philosophy, Rorty's description of the vocation of philosophy too frequently appears to endorse Weber's description of the approach many American intellectuals have adopted toward the academy: "The American's conception of the teacher is: he sells me his knowledge ... for my father's money, just as the greengrocer sells my mother cabbage."[17]

Needless to say, the implication of Rorty's prolific use of the metaphor of exchange goes well beyond the problem it might pose for his pedagogy. Recall that as a strong poet, Rorty's account of intellectual history and philosophy follows Nietzsche's definition of "truth" as "a mobile army of metaphors" (CIS 17). Intellectual history may be conceived, he argues, as the non-teleological evolution of metaphoric redescriptions. In his words, "Old metaphors are constantly dying off into

THE POLITICS OF DIFFERENCE

literalness, and then serving as a platform and foil for new metaphors" (CIS 16). The strong poets of history are those persons who develop new vocabularies as tools "for doing things which could not even have been envisaged before these tools were available" (CIS 17).

Given the elemental role of metaphors in Rorty's analysis, however, his own use of the economic appears to be a rechauffe at best. As a tool of description, it certainly captures an important part of contemporary liberalism. But, it hardly provides a way of "doing new things never evisaged before." Rather, it seems to support doing the same old things in a way only too frequently envisaged in the American polity. Indeed, for many, to "cash in" on the American dream is the very "essence" of American romance.

The peculiarly American feature of Rorty's romance is not, however, simply confined to his use of economic metaphors. Rather, on a more general level, his metaphoric strategy reflects some of the characteristics that Alexis de Tocqueville first associated with American philosophy:

To treat tradition as valuable for information only and to accept existing facts as no more than a useful sketch to show how things could be done differently and better...such are the principal characteristics of American philosophy (DA. II. 429).[18]

Unlike either Arendt's vision of the loss of American political freedom or Bloom's *Closing of the American Mind*, Rorty criticizes those romances which yearn for, to use his own phrase, "a world well lost." Rather, as we have just seen, Rorty views the past itself as a series of ossified metaphors that provide the platform for developing alternate vocabularies which "show how things could be done differently and better."

65

Concentrating on these old metaphors, Rorty often wages his attack on the "metaphysical" commitments of the past. As indicated, however, he can successfully dismiss these "metaphysical" ideas only by interpreting their metaphorical structure, literally. That is, he must interpret them as if they were actually offering a description of the way the world *really* is. But, as Plato might have been the first to admit, these "ideas" are not to be taken literally. After all, he has Socrates' remind us, they are cultural artifacts of human creation; part of the story we tell about ourselves. In contrast to Plato's Socrates, the danger of being persuaded by Rorty's analysis is that we may lose the cultural and political significance and value of such stories by being overly concerned with whether or not they are metaphysical.

But, once we drop the idea that it matters whether a narrative is "metaphysical" or not, we can no doubt offer a reading of our cultural history that is more complex than one that tells of the triumph of "good" pragmatics over "bad" metaphysical ideas. As Plato might have been the first to admit, these "ideas" are, after all, cultural artifacts of human creation; part of the story we tell about ourselves. It might be therapeutic to remind us of this occasionally, but by focusing on whether a text is metaphysical or not, we may lose the cultural and political significance and value of such stories.

According to Michael Walzer, the diverse understandings of a culture "are frequently expressed in general concepts — in [a people's] historical ideals, its public rhetoric, its foundational texts, its ceremonies and rituals. It is not only what people do but how they explain and justify what they do, the stories they tell, the principles they invoke, that constitute a moral culture." Because of the complexity and plurality entailed in this conception of ethical life, Walzer concludes, "cultures are always open to the possibility of conflict and contradiction."[19]

To illustrate Walzer's point, we might consider the alternative vocabularies we use in our cultural and political practices. For example, in defining the differences between "liberal" and "democratic" uses of liberty, Isaiah Berlin has claimed that,

the desire to be governed by myself, or at any rate to participate in the process by which my life is to be controlled, may be as deep a wish as that of a free area of action, and perhaps historically older. But it is not a desire for the same thing. So different is it, indeed, as to have led in the end to the great clash of ideologies that dominates our world.[20]

In defense of moral pluralism, Rorty follows Berlin in arguing against all "telic conceptions of human perfection." In approaching such metaphysical conceptions, Berlin warns: "To block before man every door but one, no matter how noble the prospect upon which it opens... is to sin against the truth that he is a man a being with a life of his own" (127).

However noble his own remarks, as contingent, our vocabularies of freedom are not, of course, restricted to Berlin's conceptual scheme. Indeed, as pluralistic, our linguistic uses of "liberty" and "freedom" are often conjugated in terms of our distinct cultural and historical understandings of such values as "agency," "autonomy," "democracy," "community," and "virtue." As historically complex, these distinct conceptions of liberty are often appropriate to different spheres of our historically developed discursive and cultural practices.

By conflating the differences preserved in our use of such terms as "liberty," "freedom," and "democracy," however, Rorty ironically transforms one of the elemental conflicts within our political culture into yet another romantic presentation of good texts over bad texts; human sanctity over philosophical sin; and freedom over enslavement. In this way, the irony, contingency and complexity of ethical life may require a greater respect for difference than is sometimes found in Rorty's liberal romance.

NOTES

1. Altarity (Chicago: University Press, 1987), p. xxi.

2. Unless otherwise indicated, translations of Hegel's work will be based on the following editions:

HP   *Lectures on the History of Philosophy*, trans. Haldane (London: Kegan Paul, 1895), 3 volumes.

LA   *Lectures on Aesthetics*, trans. Knox (Oxford: University Press, 1975), 2 volumes.

PS   *Phenomenology of Spirit*, trans. A.V. Miller (Oxford: University Press, 1981)*

PR   *Philosophy of Right*, trans. Knox (Oxford: University Press, 1942)*

[* Citations refer to paragraph rather than page number]

3. In terms of the comic dimensions of its subject, then, while Hegel's work reflects the narrative structure of the Commedia, it may share more in common with, let us say, Aquinas' Summa Theologiae than with Dante's unique pilgrimage toward a personal vision of universal salvation.

4. Oxford Lectures on Poetry (London: MacMillan, 1965), p. 70.

5. "The Argument of Comedy" in English Institute Essays (New York: Columbia University Press, 1949), p. 455.

6. Tragedy and Comedy, p. 20-22.

7. Fragility of Goodness, p. 68.

8. Kundera, The Book of Laughter and Forgetting, trans. Michael Henry Heim (London: Penguin, 1978), p. 8.

9. Metahistory (Baltimore: Johns Hopkins University Press, 1973, p. 8.

10. All citations are from Taylor's "Paralectics" Center for Advanced Study, University of Virginia, March 22, 1989.

11. Irony, Contingency and Solidarity (Cambridge: Cambridge University Press, 1989), p. 11.

12. "Unger, Castoriadis, and the Romance of a National Future." Northwestern University Law Review, 82 (Winter 1988), 343.

13. "Thugs and Theorists." Political Theory 15 (November 1987), 567.

14. Consequences of Pragmatism (Minneapolis: University of Minnesota Press, 1982), p. 165.

15. Contest of Faculties (London: Methuen, 1985), p. 153.

16. Goethe once complained, "I wish I knew when Plato was being ironic and when he wasn't." The same might be said of Goethe, Plato and Rorty.

While I agree with Rorty that Plato's placement of philosophy at the center of the city may be politically dangerous, I am questioning Rorty's prevailing metaphor. See below.

17. "Science as a Vocation," in *From Max Weber*, trans. Gerth and Mills (Oxford: Oxford University Press, 1946).

18. *Democracy in America* (New York: Anchor, 1969), II, 429.

19. *Interpretation and Social Criticism* (Cambridge, Mass.: Harvard University Press, 1987), p. 29.

20. *Four Essays on Liberty*, p. 127.

21. For example, see: Flathman's discussion in T*he Philosophy and Politics of Freedom*, (Chicago: University of Chicago Press, 1987) and Pitkin, "Are Freedom and Liberty Twins?" *Political Theory*, 16 (Nov. 1988), 523-553.

V
COMMENTS ON TAYLOR'S
"PARALECTICS"

RICHARD RORTY
PROFESSOR OF HUMANITIES
UNIVERSITY OF VIRGINIA

THE GOD OF THE PHILOSOPHERS

Pascal earned himself a footnote in the theology books by distinguishing between the God of Abraham, Isaac, and Jacob and the God of the philosophers. Since Pascal's time, the former God has remained about the same. But the latter God has gotten weirder and weirder, as philosophy has gotten less and less relevant to the religious believer's hopes and fears.

The God of Abraham, Isaac, and Jacob is in more or less friendly rivalry with the God of Matthew, Mark, and Luke, the one testified to by Mohammed, the God testified to by Joseph Smith, and a lot of others. These Gods are all in the same line of business. They all deal in the same products: hopes of heaven, hopes of seeing one's enemies fry in hell, and fear of going to hell oneself. They are the gods of religious believers, as opposed to the theologians.

This distinction between religious believers and theologians is a distinction between people who, when they think about God, immediately think about their own personal immortality, and those who think personal immortality largely irrelevant to God-talk. On my (loaded) definition, you are not a religious believer unless you think that you will survive death pretty much as you are, complete with parts and passions, and will then have dealings with a God who is built pretty much like you, only with bigger parts and passions. The outcome of these dealings will be largely determined by your success, prior to death, in making the right choice among the competing deities.

Theologians, by contrast, think that they can avoid a choice among these various Gods. They are eclectic, in the sense that they are prepared to dress *any* of the rival deities up in the same theoretical clothing. They are syncretic, in that they find all their customers indistinguishable once they have donned their new outfit — for this outfit conceals whatever idiosyncratic parts or passions the customers may have. Their main interest is in the up-to-dateness of the styles of clothing which they offer. They care more about staying ahead of the other theologians than about who their customers are. They care more about the purity and rigor of their designs than about their own personal fates. In private, at least, they tend to agree with the old-fashioned naturalistic atheists like me that when you die you rot.

The theologians read the philosophers in the way in which couturiers in underdeveloped portions of the fashion world read the latest reports from Paris. For their activity consists largely in changing the label on the latest philosophical costume. The new label always reads "God," no matter what the old label was. Forty years ago, Tillich relabeled what Heidegger called "Being" as God. Nowadays, Professor Taylor and his fellow a/theologians are relabeling Derrida's "différance."

A/THEOLOGY

Professor Taylor's book *Erring* has "A Postmodern A/theology" as its subtitle. There is a slash between "A" and "theology," a slash which marks the difference between my old-fashioned kind of atheism and Prof. Taylor's new kind. That slash is, *so zu singen*, not only the rat in *rature*, the *Riß* in *Umriß*, and the neatly combed and slicked-down part in *partage*, but also the ecstatic ooh! in *ousia*, the serpent's hiss in history, the nostalgic sigh in *Seiendheit*, and the *Besser-wisser* in *Gewissenhabenwollen*.

This slash is a trademark of a theologian who, just as a philosopher is congratulating himself on finally having wiggled out from under all those heaps of dirty satin and chiffon, the discarded old clothes of what Heidegger called the "ontotheological tradition," sneaks up behind him and pops an all-enveloping, one-size-fits-all cloak over his head. On the back of this cloak are written, in letters of pale shimmering fire, the cryptic words "Now at your nearby tailor's! For the first time ever! The ultimate Vestment of Godhead! Guaranteed self-deconstructing and self-repairing!"

Heidegger, starting off in 1924 with the claim that "all philosophical research is atheism," spent a lot of his time describing Christianity as a crucial stage in the disastrous forgetfulness of what he called "Being." Heidegger thought he had a patent on "Being," but then Tillich began marketing it in America under the label "object of ultimate concern." Tillich claimed that Christianity's symbol of this concern was better than anybody else's. It was better because, as Kierkegaard pointed out, it came equipped with the blatantly self-contradictory doctrine of Incarnation. The advantages of this doctrine were summed up by the Duke of Wellington when greeted by a bank clerk in Hyde Park with the words "Mr. Smith, I believe." The Duke rejoined, "If you can believe *that*, you can believe *anything*." One imagines the same reply being made by the non-spatiotemporally-locatable Creator of Heaven and Earth upon being hailed with the name of the prophet from Nazareth.

Tillich would have treated such a riposte from his Creator as a compliment rather than a rebuke. He saw that any theology which admits to its own unmediatable self-contradictoriness, and thus is able to stitch in whatever "other to Reason" philosophy comes up with, has a big edge on the competition. Heidegger was at first indignant with such appropriations of his patented design, but he later learned to relax and enjoy it. In his last

73

years, he was even heard to murmur things like "Only a God can save us Now." He eventually came to display the same avuncular attitude toward admiring theologians as toward admiring physicists like von Weizsäcker and admiring poets like Celan.

Taylor, if I grasp his project correctly, is playing Tillich to Derrida's Heidegger. He brushes aside Derrida's claim that deconstruction "blocks every relationship to theology" in the same way that Tillich brushed aside Heidegger's identification of philosophical research with atheism. I suspect that Taylor will have the same success in recloaking Derrida that Tillich had in recloaking Heidegger. Indeed, there are signs that Derrida is beginning to relax and enjoy the transvestite role in which Taylor has cast him. Lately Derrida has been suggesting, to my astonishment and dismay, that there is an ethical-political-religious point to deconstruction. This suggestion is likely to help Taylor's chances as the operator of one of the many American franchises for Derridean thought.

NATURALIZING DERRIDA

Since I like Derrida's style a lot better than Heidegger's, I am glad that Taylor and his friends are taking theology off in a Derridean direction. If we are going to have theologians at all, it will be nice to have theologians with a sense of humor, a faculty in which Heidegger was notably deficient. But, as the old-fashioned kind of atheist, the kind without the slash, I keep wishing that we didn't have any theologians. I wish we could stop running together the needs of religious believers with the needs of the philosophers. I would especially like to separate the believer's need to put oneself under the protection of someone bigger than himself for the sake of post-mortem happiness and revenge on his enemies, from the philosopher's need to find a theoretical vocabulary more comprehensive than those of her predecessors.

This is why, in the day-to-day operation of my own little Derrida franchise, I do my best to "block any relation" between Derrida and theology. I try to assimilate him to Wittgenstein and to Dewey — and thus, indirectly, to Dewey's masters, Hegel and Darwin. I want, as Taylor says, "Hegelianism without absolute knowledge," just as Dewey did. Dewey, on my reading, took from Darwin the idea that world-history wasn't going to converge to a point at which Subject and Object came together. Instead, it will expand forever, as new forms of intellectual and personal and political life are invented to replace old ones — proliferating rather than converging. Philosophy will go on forever, with ever fatter breeds of dogmatic cat being savaged by newly evolved, ever leaner and meaner, species of skeptical rat. But it will never find rest; it will never find a peaceable kingdom where the cats and the rats can lie down together. Still, with luck it might leave theology behind, just as politico-economic forms of life in most parts of the world have been able, thanks to modern technology, to leave human slavery behind.

I see the motive power of this engine of perpetual renewal and proliferation as the random occurrence, in the occasional human mind, of new words in which to describe people, or societies, or the universe. Euripides, Plato, St. Paul, Newton, Goethe, Hegel, Darwin, Marx, Dewey, Kafka, Heidegger, and Derrida are examples of such occurrences. The occasional intrusion of the Otherness which such figures instantiate keeps things changing—sometimes for the better, sometimes for the worse. So although I agree with Taylor that we need constant doses of Otherness to keep us on our toes, to keep our dialogues from turning monological, I don't want to locate the source of this Otherness in something bigger than ourselves. As a good naturalist, I take the source of this occasional irruption of Otherness to be simply some curious neural kink, or odd psycho-sexual twist, or genetic mini-mutation. On my view, there is nothing more to Otherness than the random events which produce random effects on our language, and thus on poetry, politics, and philosophy.

My objection to the Other with a capital O, Language with a capital L, and Différance with a capital D is the same as my objection to Being with a capital B: all such capitalizations tempt us to look outside of time and space, outside of the contingent workings of nature, for salvation. No matter how much a/theologians protest that this is not what they have in mind, that seems to me the effect of their work. They help re-enslave us to the thought that we are, or can get, under the protection of Something or Somebody Bigger Than Ourselves. That is the distinctively theological motif in a/theology which I want to resist. So I do my best to read Derrida as a prophet of Contingency rather than of Otherness, and to make him over into a genial, what-the-hell, 19th-century kind of atheist, instead of a postmodern slasher.

A FEW REBUTTALS

I shall end by taking up three of the terrible things Taylor says about me and trying to rebut them.

(a) Taylor glosses my remark that we enter relationships with other people in order to become new beings as the claim that "the relation to an 'other' is, therefore, a self-relation that is self transforming. The 'other' is not really other but is actually a *moment* in *my* own self-becoming" (p. 17). This seems to me like saying that if you want to be other than you are, you are therefore desiring to be the same as you already are, because what you already are is somebody who desires otherness. That, in turn, seems an updated version of the claim that if you strive to be free from sin, you are thereby sinning the sin of pride, always already offending God by daring

76

to strive for what only His Grace can effect. I don't see how to get away from such pointless paradoxes except by dropping Great Big Ideas like "Self," "Other," "Sin," and "Grace," and substituting little ideas about our hopes for little changes. Such little, concrete ideas help us express our hope to become a new being *gradually* and dialectically, one bit at a time. Such a preference for dialectics expresses, I think, our hope to be changed by conversation with fellow finite mortals, rather than by the intrusion of a nonspatiotemporal agent.

(b) Taylor quotes Derrida as saying that "play must be conceived of before the alternative of presence and absence," and as prophesying the birth of a "formless, mute, infant, and terrifying form of monstrosity." He suggests that my insights make me blind to these passages. I don't think they make me blind to them, but they certainly make me dislike them. I think they show Derrida either exhibiting the nostalgia for which he rebukes Heidegger, or at his pseudo-prophetic worst. Such passages mark the upsurge, in Derrida's usually good-humored prose, of that old sado-masochistic resentment which Nietzsche warned us against. I hate it when philosophers — like Nietzsche at *his* worst — rub their hands together and announce the imminence of monstrous births. I hate it even more when they hint that what they are really looking forward to is being nibbled to death by rats. Compared to the latter desire, even a hope for martyrdom by crucifixion seems reasonably sane.

(c) Taylor calls me a "cultural imperialist" for saying that "truth and justice lie in the direction marked by the successive stages of *European* thought." "Imperialist" is a fighting word, in the sense that it suggests images of the Conquistadores' horses and of Gatling guns. But I bet that Taylor too thinks that truth lies in the direction that leads away from Aristotle toward Darwin, and that justice lies in the direction that leads away from Marsilius of Padua and toward John Stuart Mill. If he can find an Indian Darwin or a Chinese Mill, fine. But I suspect that, like Derrida's and mine, his sense of what is possible and important is what it is because he was fed on a European intellectual diet. I see no point in pretending that we can rise to a level of abstraction from which the differences between this guy who was half-god and half-elephant and Plato's *pharmakon* become invisible. Hoping to avoid cultural imperialism by rising to that level seems to me as vain as the hope of avoiding monologue by anthropomorphizing, or ratifying, the Other.

I suspect that my attempts at rebuttal will merely suggest to Taylor that the story of the Giant Rats of Paris is one for which I am not yet spiritually prepared. Nevertheless, I am grateful to him for giving me the opportunity to advertise the services of my own franchise operation. We naturalistic Derrideans pride ourselves on our use of advanced philosophical technology to stop up onto-theological ratholes. Give us a try.

1. The Daribi, located in highland New Guinea, are the people among whom P Wagner conducted fieldwork.

WORKING PAPERS SERIES

Other Working Papers published by the Committee on Comparative Study of Individual and Society include:

Working Paper No. I: Critique of Modernity

Edited by Robert W. Langbaum
October 1986

Working Paper No. 2: Issues in Compensatory Justice:
The Bhopal Accident
Edited by R.S. Khare
June 1987

Working Paper No. 3: Perspectives on Islamic Law,
Justice and Society

Edited by R.S. Khare
September 1987

Working Paper No. 4: Issues in Evolution, History
and Progress

Edited by Robert P. Scharlemann
June 1990

DATE DUE

JUN 2 0 1994			
			Printed in USA